British Radicalism and the French Revolution 1789–1815

H. T. DICKINSON

Basil Blackwell

Copyright © H. T. Dickinson 1985

First published 1985
Reprinted 1988

Basil Blackwell Ltd
108 Cowley Road, Oxford OX4 1JF, UK

Basil Blackwell Inc.
432 Park Avenue South, Suite 1503
New York, NY 10016, USA

British Library Cataloguing in Publication Data

Dickinson, H.T.
    British radicalism and the French Revolution, 1789–1815.—(Historical
    Association studies)
    1. Radicalism—Great Britain—History—18th century. 2. Radicalism—
    Great Britain—History—19th century
    I. Title   II. Series
    320.5'3'0941   HN400.R3

    ISBN 0–631–13945–1 ✓

Library of Congress Cataloging in Publication Data

Dickinson, H. T.
    British radicalism and the French revolution, 1789–1815.
    (Historical Association studies)
    Bibliography: p.
    Includes index.
    1. Great Britain—Politics and government—1789–1820.
    2. Jacobins—England—History. 3. Radicalism—England—
    History—18th century. 4. Radicalism—England—History—
    19th century. 5. France—History—Revolution, 1789–1799–
    Influence. I. Title. II. Series.
    DA520.D53   1985   944.04   84–28330

ISBN 0–631–13945–1 (pbk.)

Typeset by Cambrian Typesetters, Frimley, Surrey
Printed in Great Britain by Whitstable Litho Ltd, Whitstable, Kent

Contents

Preface

This short study is expressly designed for students and hence it concentrates on those questions which have aroused the greatest debate among historians and on which students need most guidance. No attempt has been made to provide a detailed chronological narrative or to examine all aspects of British radicalism in the years between 1789 and 1815. The first chapter explores the extent to which the new radical societies of the 1790s differed in their organization, their ideology and their methods from those of earlier reformers. The second chapter examines the forces of reaction which triumphed over the radicals and suggests that government repression was not the only or even perhaps the most significant reason for this success. After briefly noting the insurrectionary conspiracies in Ireland, the third chapter investigates the extent to which a revolutionary movement existed in Britain and questions how far the revolutionaries were implicated in the economic protests of the period. The gradual revival of radicalism in the early 1800s is the subject of the last chapter and the analysis here concentrates on measuring the ideological and organizational changes made by the reformers during these years. The list of references indicates sources and offers guidance to further reading.

H. T. Dickinson

1 The British Jacobins

Origins and Influences

From its dramatic first months in 1789, and for many years to follow, the French Revolution stimulated intense political debate within Britain and deeply polarized public opinion on the question of reforming the British constitution. It did not, however, create all of the circumstances which gave rise to demands for political reform. The social and economic transformation of Britain gave birth to radicalism well before 1789. Nor was the French Revolution the sole influence on the political aims, the ideology or the methods of those radicals who were soon to be referred to as the British Jacobins. The British radicals of the 1790s drew many of their ideas and some of their inspiration from a long tradition of hostility to the ruling oligarchy and criticism of the aristocratic social hierarchy of eighteenth-century Britain.

By the later eighteenth century, major social and economic developments within Britain were combining to create a growing body of opinion critical of the power and the policies of the aristocratic elite. These changes had their greatest effect on the political consciousness of the middling orders, especially those who lived in urban areas, but economic crisis and social dislocation were also capable of recruiting many of the skilled craftsmen and artisans into the campaign for political reform. The population of Britain was rising rapidly in the late eighteenth century and much of this increase was concentrated in the larger urban centres. London grew to contain nearly one million inhabitants, while Birmingham, Bristol, Edinburgh, Glasgow, Leeds, Liverpool, Manchester and Southwark all increased to between 50,000 and 85,000 inhabitants. A further ten towns grew to between 25,000 and 50,000 inhabitants, and at least twenty more had a population of over 10,000. Population growth and urban expansion were sustained by significant economic expansion in agriculture, commerce and industry. These changes in turn produced a growing middle class whose advancing wealth and

1

improved education inspired demands for greater social status and political influence. Many of the middling orders resented their dependence upon the landed elite whose policies could have a profound effect on their economic welfare. Political weakness had economic consequences since the burden of taxation was steadily shifted from the shoulders of the great landowners onto those who produced, sold or used many items of popular consumption. Furthermore, government policies could result in wars which dislocated trade or in legislative restrictions on the activities of traders and manufacturers. These grievances were felt quite low down the social scale, among small shopkeepers, tradesmen and artisans. Even the labouring poor could express violent resentment of the ruling elite, because they were not protected from rising prices and declining wages, especially when these could be traced directly to the selfishness of their employers or the particular policies of the governing classes.

As the population of many towns grew substantially during the eighteenth century, and as their economy was transformed, so the political culture of these urban centres expanded in range and grew in sophistication. This burgeoning political culture enabled the middling orders in particular to establish their own independent organizations, to inform themselves about public affairs and to develop advanced notions of their political rights and liberties. Clubs and societies enabled the middling orders to combine in mutual support and to organize themselves independently of the patrician elite. The members of these associations learned to organize their own activities without resorting to aristocratic leadership. They gradually became critical of the governing elite and ultimately used these institutions as vehicles for co-ordinating campaigns to challenge the political influence of their social superiors. At first designed primarily for social and entertainment purposes, these clubs and societies increasingly became educational and political. They formed a countrywide communications network which could later be exploited by political radicals.

These societies could never have become more political if their members had not absorbed a wealth of political information and a libertarian political ideology through the rapid expansion of the press. By the late eighteenth century London alone was served by thirteen daily and ten tri-weekly newspapers, while in the provinces there were over fifty weekly newspapers. Total annual sales of newspapers were as high as 12.5 million by 1775, and some 17 million by 1793. In addition there was a wealth of political information and propaganda published in the numerous monthly periodicals and in the large number of individual pamphlets produced during any political crisis. Most of the more successful publications were anti-ministerial in their politics. The flourishing and expanding press played a major role in encouraging a large public to be critical of the governing elite and to be aware of suggestions for reforming the political system. Long before the French Revolution the opponents of the governing elite had waged a propaganda campaign in the press against the growing power of the executive and the corrupt means by which the Government subverted the independence of Parliament and the liberties of the state. Regular attacks were made on crown patronage and persistent demands were made for economical reforms designed to diminish this patronage and to reduce the crown's influence over Parliament. Long before the rise of any organized radical movement outside Parliament there were demands for more frequent general elections and for the redistribution of parliamentary seats from the tiny rotten boroughs to the large unrepresented towns and the more populous counties. Long before the radicals began demanding a major extension of the franchise there were constant references in the press to the rights and liberties of Englishmen. Ever since the Glorious Revolution in 1688 the opponents of royal power and aristocratic oligarchy had asserted that all men should enjoy the benefits of the rule of law and be free from the interference of an arbitrary, tyrannical government. They insisted that all men possessed the rights to life, liberty and property, that sovereign authority rested with the people at large and that, in the last resort, all men could forcibly resist a tyrannical government.

The social and economic grievances of the middle classes, their ability to exploit a flourishing urban political culture and an active press, and their growing consciousness of their political rights, all combined to create the potential for a sustained challenge to the political dominance of the landed elite. What was needed to transform this potential into reality was a profound and prolonged political crisis which would undermine the authority of the governing classes and convince the middling orders that reforms were needed in the whole political structure. The first crisis of this nature occurred in the early decades of George III's reign when there was growing alarm at what appeared to be a deliberate campaign to increase the power of the crown by unconstitutional means. Modern historians have proved these fears to be grossly exaggerated and even entirely unwarranted, but at the time they produced prolonged ministerial instability, intense public debate on the threat to the balance of the constitution and the liberties of the subject, and determined

3

opposition to government policies at home and in the American colonies. The American colonies secured their political independence by force of arms, while within Britain a vigorous, though peaceful, opposition was mounted against the ruling oligarchy.

From the late 1760s to the early 1780s the petitioning movement led first by John Wilkes and then by the Association movement started by Christopher Wyvill sought to rally public opinion and to create extra-parliamentary organizations in an effort to reform the constitution. These reform movements exploited the press and the clubs and societies which flourished in London and the larger provincial towns. They created new political associations such as the Society of the Supporters of the Bill of Rights, the Society for Constitutional Information and various Constitutional societies and county associations. These brought political activists into contact with each other and disseminated reform propaganda to a wider public. They also organized national petitioning campaigns to demonstrate the extent of their support and to bring pressure to bear upon government and Parliament. The intense political debate in which they were engaged produced a variety of reform proposals and a more radical notion of the liberties of the subject. The more moderate reformers campaigned for the traditional demands of economical reform, in order to restrict the patronage which the executive could use to influence the composition and the decisions of Parliament. Other reformers did not believe that these policies went far enough. In their view the liberties of the subject could be defended only if Parliament were made more representative of the people as a whole. This could only be achieved by parliamentary reform. Many reformers demanded more frequent general elections or a redistribution of seats to the large towns and most populous counties, though a few went much further than this. As early as 1780 the radical leaders of the Westminister Association drafted what was to become the famous six-point programme of parliamentary reform: universal manhood suffrage, annual Parliaments, equal sized constituencies, the secret ballot, the abolition of property qualifications for MPs and the payment of MPs. Radical propagandists such as John Cartwright claimed that these radical reforms would not be revolutionary innovations, but would simply restore the democratic system of representation that had existed in the distant Anglo-Saxon past. Other radical theorists such as Richard Price rejected this appeal to England's ancient constitution. They claimed that radical parliamentary reform should be granted because a democratic system of representation was the only way to convert the natural rights of all men into civil liberties. Price and others insisted that all

4

men possessed the natural and inalienable rights to life, liberty and property and that these rights could be preserved only if all men had an equal right to elect the members of the legislature who made the laws governing their life, liberty and property.

This campaign for reform resulted in a number of bills to curtail the influence of crown patronage and even in motions in the House of Commons to achieve a moderate reform of Parliament. In 1783 a significant minority of MPs was prepared to vote for parliamentary reform and in 1785 the Prime Minister, the Younger Pitt, secured the support of 174 MPs, a significant minority, for his proposal to eliminate thirty-six of the smallest parliamentary boroughs. Clearly, the extra-parliamentary reform movement had made giant strides in a relatively short time, but it was neither firmly based nor deeply rooted. Few of the reformers were genuine democrats. Even the more committed radicals would probably have been satisfied with a franchise restricted to male householders or those paying direct taxes and rates. None of the radicals seriously expected the labouring masses to take an active role in national affairs beyond the exercise of the vote. The organizational machinery of the reform movement remained firmly in the hands of men of property and education drawn from the middling ranks of society. They resented the excessive influence of the great landowners and were determined to increase their own representation in Parliament, but they did not expect the poor to govern nor did they anticipate that poor men would actually sit in the House of Commons. Moreover, while they were prepared to reform the electoral system, they still regarded the ideal constitution as a mixture of monarchy, aristocracy and democracy achieved through the careful balance of King, Lords and Commons. There was no desire to undermine monarchical government or to abolish aristocratic privileges. Nor was there a serious campaign to alter the social hierarchy or to redistribute the nation's wealth more equitably. For nearly all the radicals the primary aim was lower taxes and cheap government. There was very little in their programme which had a direct appeal and a compelling attraction for the lower orders of society.

The ending of the American war, the rapid recovery of the economy and the restoration of political stability at home led to a sudden collapse in support for the radicals and for the cause of parliamentary reform. By the early 1790s, however, radicalism had not only revived, but had made major advances on the position which it had occupied a decade before. The movement became more radical in its ideology, more revolutionary in its aims and more influential in its impact on the masses. A number of factors contributed to this dramatic transformation, though much the most important was the outbreak of revolution in France.

The Federal Constitution of the new republic of the United States of America, ratified in 1787, demonstrated to British radicals that it was possible to erect a government according to the will of the people and in defence of their sovereignty and their natural rights. The Americans showed that political equality could be reconciled with the defence of property and the maintenance of a moderately differentiated social structure. They provided empirical evidence that a fairer representation of the people did not necessarily lead to social anarchy or civil war. The radical political consequences of the American Revolution highlighted the conservative political developments in Britain since the Glorious Revolution of 1688. This contrast was forcibly pointed out by those reformers who founded the Revolution Society in order to commemorate the centenary of the Glorious Revolution. The Revolution Society insisted that the underlying principles of 1688–9 were far more radical than later political developments would indicate. Its members insisted that the Glorious Revolution enshrined the doctrine of the sovereigny of the people. On 4 November 1789, in the most famous of the addresses given to the Revolution Society, Richard Price, the veteran reformer, asserted that the Glorious Revolution had proclaimed the most important rights inherent in the nature of free men: the right to liberty of conscience, the right to resist arbitrary tyranny, and, most radical of all, 'the right to chuse our own governors; to cashier them for misconduct; and to frame a government for ourselves'. Unfortunately, these rights had not been fully secured in 1688–9, but now was the time to achieve them. The Revolution Society, which was dominated by Dissenters, played an important role in the campaign to repeal the Test and Corporation Acts which restricted offices in central and local government to Anglicans. In waging the campaign for repeal, in press and Parliament, from 1787 to 1790 the Dissenters and their allies among the liberal Anglicans argued that liberty of conscience was a natural and inalienable right and therefore the state had no legitimate authority to impose civil disabilities on particular religious opinions. In demanding religious equality these men were led into a campaign for political liberty as the best means of securing all their natural rights.

The interest aroused by the publication of Richard Price's address to the Revolution Society, and the intensity of the parliamentary debate on the repeal of the Test and Corporation Acts in 1790, owed much to the climate of political excitement created in Britain by the dramatic and astonishing events in France. The outbreak of revolution in a country long regarded as the prime example of absolute monarchy was hailed as convincing proof that a new age of liberty was at hand. Political events in France over the succeeding years were to have an electrifying effect on British politics. The revolution was sudden and surprising; it produced a political earthquake sending seismic shocks throughout Europe. The impact on Britain was profound and was widely diffused throughout the whole of society. Within a few short months the strongest monarch in Europe was humbled by his subjects, the entrenched privileges of the aristocracy were condemned, the church was placed under secular control, the inalienable rights of man were proclaimed, and a representative assembly was charged with drawing up a new constitution. British reformers of all shades of opinion were galvanized into action. John Cartwright declared: 'The French, Sir, are not only asserting their own rights, but they are advancing the general liberties of mankind.' Richard Price proclaimed: 'What an eventful period is this! I am thankful that I have lived to see . . . the rights of men better understood than ever: and nations panting for liberty, which seemed to have lost the idea of it . . . I see the ardour for liberty catching and spreading; a general amendment beginning in human affairs' (Dickinson, 1977, p. 236).

Events in France stimulated the campaign in Britain for the repeal of the Test and Corporation Acts, encouraged the Revolution Society to send an address of congratulation to the French National Assembly on 4 November 1789, and revived the Society of Constitutional Information (SCI) which had been moribund for some years. Daniel Adams, its hard-working secretary, built up membership and even attracted a few men of more humble origin such as William Sharp, an engraver, and Thomas Holcroft, a cobbler. The SCI resumed its dissemination of radical publications, established political contacts throughout the country and revived its enquiry into the state of parliamentary representation in England and Wales. This eventually led to the publication in 1792 of T. H. B. Oldfield's *History of the Boroughs*, which provided the evidence vital to the effective denunciation of the system of representation. In March 1790 one of the most distinguished members of the SCI, Henry Flood, introduced a motion in the House of Commons to strip all rotten boroughs of one of their representatives, to give an additional 100 seats to the counties and to extend the franchise to resident householders. In an impressive speech, Flood argued that developments in France had made reform at home more urgent than ever – though he claimed that the excesses in France could be avoided in Britain by timely concessions to the propertied middle classes.

7

Flood failed to gain much support in Parliament, but events in France did inspire a minority of opposition Whigs to dedicate themselves to moderate political reform. On 14 July 1790 the Whig Club organized a monster reform banquet to celebrate Bastille Day. Over 650 friends of liberty attended. Resolutions were passed rejoicing at the establishment of liberty in France and pledging support for parliamentary reform at home. Although this meeting alarmed Edmund Burke, and helped to drive a wedge between conservative and liberal Whigs, some of the latter continued their support for political change. In April 1792 some liberal Whigs established the Society of the Friends of the People and proclaimed their support for moderate reform as a means of averting the disasters which were befalling France at this time. Using the researches of Oldfield one of its members, George Tierney, produced a 'Report on the State of the Representation of England and Wales'. This evidence was used by the liberal Whigs when they tried in vain to secure a parliamentary Reform Bill in 1793 and 1797.

There can be no doubt about the importance of the political events in France in reviving the interest in reform within Britain of such veteran radicals as John Cartwright, Richard Price, Christopher Wyvill and John Horne Tooke. The French Revolution stimulated the Revolution Society to new efforts, awoke the sleeping SCI, and encouraged the liberal element among the Whigs to renewed efforts at economical reform and moderate parliamentary reform. The greatest impact of the French Revolution however was on the new and more radical societies which sprang up in London and the provinces in the early 1790s. Often referred to as the British Jacobins, these radicals made advances in organization, extended their membership further down the social scale, advanced more revolutionary aims, and developed new means of achieving their objectives. The French Revolution aroused these men to political action and provided them with ideas about redressing their grievances, but it was the economic circumstances of the 1790s which enabled them on occasion to recruit mass support. The French Revolution did not simply set a political example for the oppressed people of Europe. The disturbed state of Europe in 1792–3 led to an economic depression in Britain, resulting in widespread unemployment and lower wages. Foreign trade and domestic manufacture were increasingly dislocated by the long, bitter and enormously expensive military conflict which broke out between Britain and France in early 1793. The war not only seriously interrupted trade, but placed a steadily growing tax burden on the middling and lower orders as vast sums were raised by indirect taxes on items of popular consumption. Economic distress reached critical proportions in 1795–6. Severe harvest failure pushed up food prices to record levels at a time when the poor were already faced with lower wages and higher taxes. Throughout the 1790s, but particularly in the years 1792–6, distress was a major recruiting agent for the radical cause.

Organization and Composition

By far the most important of the new radical societies was the London Corresponding Society (LCS). This body was founded on 25 January 1792, when a mere nine men, led by Thomas Hardy, a humble shoemaker, met at the Bell tavern in the Strand to discuss the economic distress and high prices of the day. Eight of the men agreed to establish a society which would meet once a week, and would levy a subscription of one penny at each meeting. Thomas Hardy was chosen as the first secretary and treasurer, while Maurice Margarot, a lawyer, soon became the first president. Although initially concerned about the poverty facing many of the lower orders, the LCS adopted a political programme as the remedy for their grievances. Its members dedicated themselves to universal manhood suffrage, annual elections and the redistribution of parliamentary seats from the rotten boroughs to the large towns. Hardy and his friends endeavoured to spread their ideas across London and throughout the country. They achieved rapid and quite remarkable success. Branches or divisions were set up throughout the metropolitan area. Each one was expected to recruit a minimum of thirty members. Recruits above this number were to be entered into a supernumerary book and when sixteen had been enrolled in this way a new division was started. In fact, many divisions exceeded the suggested maximum; division two, the most active of all, had nearly 700 members by late 1795. When the Seditious Meetings Act of 1795 banned political meetings of fifty or more persons, however, the LCS had a structure which could survive this restriction.

By May 1792 there were nine divisions of the LCS, each sending a delegate to the general committee which met each Thursday evening. The divisions elected their secretary and their delegate every three months. The general committee elected a smaller executive committee consisting of a secretary, president and six ordinary members. This executive committee co-ordinated the activities and policies of the LCS. Its members met two or three times each week and so the leading activists in the LCS were busy with political meetings for four or five evenings in the week. As the LCS spread over a wider area, this imposed travel problems on its

9

members; consequently it was decided to divide London into four geographical districts and to insert a district committee between the divisions and the general committee. Members of the district committee were also elected by the divisions. Thus, by 1795, the LCS possessed a sophisticated organizational structure designed to overcome the legal, financial and geographical restrictions on its political activities (Collins, 1954).

It is difficult to establish the exact size of the LCS or the precise social composition of its membership. No complete list of members exists and some distinction needs to be made between the hard-core of activists and the occasional attenders of its branch meetings. It is clear for example that some divisions were very active and well attended, whereas others had an uncertain and intermittent existence. Perhaps only half of the divisions bothered to elect delegates to the general committee. The LCS claimed a total membership of around 5,000, and this has been accepted by many historians. The latest estimates on active as distinct from total membership, however, suggests that the LCS attracted about 650 regular members to its meetings by late 1792, that this number remained stagnant throughout 1793, fluctuated between 250 and 1,000 during the next eighteen months, but then reached its peak in the second half of 1795. Despite the repressive measures of the Government, the LCS attracted a weekly attendance of over 1,500 members in the autumn of 1795, and during one week some 3,576 members attended divisional meetings. The total active membership during these weeks was probably around 3,000, but this was reduced to no more than 2,000 by the spring of 1796, and to 1,000 by the end of the year. By 1797 the active membership had shrunk to around 600, and in 1798, before its enforced dissolution, the LCS was reduced to about 400 active members (Thale, 1983, pp. xxiii–iv). Obviously the LCS could attract many more sympathizers to its large open-air meetings, and its programme was approved by a large number of people who were not members. Nonetheless, the LCS cannot be regarded as a truly mass society which drew to its weekly meetings a significant proportion of the labouring poor of the capital.

Most historians have been content, without having any detailed evidence, to describe the membership of the LCS as being largely made up of tradesmen and artisans. Certainly some of the most famous activists were tradesmen: Thomas Hardy and John Ashley were shoemakers, Francis Place a tailor, Benjamin and John Binns had been plumbers, and Richard Hodgson a hatter. On the other hand, evidence about a higher proportion of the LCS activists presents a rather different picture. One analysis of 347 activists reveals that about half of them were tradesmen or artisans. They included forty-three shoemakers or men in allied trades, twenty-seven men connected with weaving, twenty-four in the tailoring trade, fourteen watchmakers, seven carpenters, seven cabinet makers, etc. Very few of these men appear to have had a formal education, but they had managed to educate themselves moderately well. The other activists in this sample however were of a higher social status. They included eight attorneys, eight medical men, ten booksellers, eleven clerks and a variety of shopkeepers (Thale, 1983, p. xix). Another sample of some sixty-one leading activists in the LCS reveals that only sixteen men can be clearly described as artisans or tradesmen. The rest were largely made up of booksellers, printers, publishers, authors and men in the legal or medical professions. They included such leading members as John Bone, Robert Crossfield, Daniel Isaac Eaton, Joseph Gerrald, John Gale Jones, Maurice Margarot, Thomas Spence and John Thelwall (Lottes, 1979, pp. 360–73). Artisans and tradesmen clearly played a significant, but not a dominant, role in the leadership of the LCS. Among the branch activists and the rank and file members the proportion of artisans and tradesmen was no doubt much greater, but there is no evidence that the LCS ever had much appeal for unskilled labourers or the very poor. The LCS was not a genuine proletarian society despite the accusations of its enemies and the claims of some historians.

Radical organizations of this kind were not confined to London. In many ways the most radical and most interesting of the rash of provincial societies which sprang up was the Sheffield Society for Constitutional Information which was founded in November or December (it is not clear which) 1791. As with the LCS a general climate of economic unrest and an intense interest in political events in France inspired a few activists to establish a society to advance the cause of radical parliamentary reform. Within a few months the Sheffield SCI had grown from a handful of men to hundreds of members meeting in different taverns and public houses across the town. The total membership was over 1,500 by March 1792, and about 2,500 by June 1792, but the active membership was much lower than this, perhaps around 600. Members met weekly in their local branches or divisions and each group elected a delegate to a general executive committee which distributed political literature, organized petitions, communicated with the LCS and SCI in London and advised radical groups in such neighbouring towns as Leeds, Derby, Nottingham and Stockport.

The most famous members of the Sheffield SCI were Joseph Gales,

11

the publisher of the *Sheffield Register*, Henry Redhead Yorke, a travelling agitator of independent means, and William Broomhead, a master cutler. Most of the active members appear to have been small masters and skilled journeymen engaged as cutlers, filesmiths, razor makers, etc. in the small workshops of the Sheffield steel industry. Like many members of the LCS, these men were facing adverse economic circumstances made worse by the European crisis sparked off by the French Revolution. Distress helped the radicals to secure nearly 4,000 signatures on a petition for parliamentary reform in the spring of 1793, and to attract between 5,000 and 6,000 people to an open-air meeting on 28 February 1794, when resolutions were passed in favour of peace abroad and liberty at home (Seaman, 1957).

Radical societies sprang up in other large provincial towns, some of them influenced by the older reform societies and some by the examples of the LCS and the Sheffield SCI. A Constitutional Society appeared in Manchester as early as October 1790. Its leading members were Thomas Walker, a cotton merchant, and Thomas Cooper, a barrister and chemist. These men were much influenced by older reformers such as James Burgh and Joseph Priestley and they modelled their society on the London SCI. Meetings were held only once a month, when 50 to 100 men – mainly from the middle classes – met to discuss the printing and distribution of radical propaganda. For a year, from March 1792 to March 1793, this society published an excellent weekly newspaper, the *Manchester Herald*. The dramatic increase in radical fervour in 1792 led to the creation of the Patriotic Society in May and the Reformation Society in June. These societies attracted artisans, tradesmen and even a few labourers. For a few months they co-operated with the Constitutional Society in campaigning for parliamentary reform before the conservative reaction of 1793 undermined their efforts (Handforth, 1956). In Norwich the radical cause developed along similar lines. A Revolution Society set up in 1788, and dominated by middle class Dissenters, merchants and professional men, gave a lead to the reform movement. It was joined by a number of more radical clubs set up by artisans, tradesmen and shopkeepers in 1792. The political leadership of the radicals passed to these new societies who sent delegates to fortnightly meetings (Jewson, 1975). At about the same time, similar radical societies sprang up in many other towns including Birmingham, Derby, Leeds, Leicester, Nottingham, Newcastle, Stockport, Edinburgh, Dundee and Stirling. They were nearly all composed of small merchants, professional men, shopkeepers and tradesmen. Regular meetings were held in local taverns and their activities were publicized in the local newspapers. Many of these societies were quite small, attracting only a few dozen regular members, and most of them were shortlived as they felt the blast of a powerful conservative reaction in 1793. In Birmingham the Constitutional Society, which had been moribund since the mid-1780s, revived under the leadership of the veteran reformer Joseph Priestley. Its appeal was principally to professional men, middle-class merchants and manufacturers, and prosperous Dissenters. It was too moderate for men such as John Harrison, a Sheffield razor maker, who founded the Birmingham SCI in November 1792 and established contact with the LCS. But neither moderate nor radical reformers could achieve political dominance in Birmingham. A petition in favour of universal manhood suffrage only secured 2,720 signatures in May 1793, and by 1795 radicalism had withered in Birmingham. In Leicester too the reformers were divided between the moderate and more prosperous members of the Revolution Society, and the radical and more humble recruits of the Constitutional Society, but both groups soon faced strong opposition from the forces of conservative reaction and they ceased their activities by the end of 1795. Some substantial provincial towns, including Bristol, Hull, Liverpool, Plymouth and Portsmouth, could not sustain radical societies as large or even as shortlived as these. Clearly the cause of radical parliamentary reform had more support than ever before in the early 1790s, and it made impressive advances among urban artisans and tradesmen in some areas, but it failed to rally support across the whole country or within all social groups in the nation.

Aims and Assumptions

The British Jacobins of the 1790s adopted the more extreme political programme of the earlier reformers, particularly the famous six points of parliamentary reform first advocated by the Westminster Association in 1780. In their addresses, resolutions and petitions, the LCS and the provincial societies concentrated on universal manhood suffrage, annual general elections and equal parliamentary constituencies. In an Address to the Nation, published on 16 August 1792, the LCS advocated 'annually elected Parliaments, unbiassed and unbought elections, and an equal representation of the whole body of the people' (Thale, 1983, p. 18). There was widespread agreement among the British Jacobins that the right to vote should be attached to the person and not to the property of man. To deny any man the franchise was to cast a slur on his moral character and to assert that he was less than a man. The possession of wealth was no proof of

13

moral worth or civic virtue, and nor was poverty any evidence of the lack of these qualities. Many of the radical societies maintained that the claim of all subjects to the vote was a traditional right exercised long ago under England's ancient constitution. The six points of parliamentary reform would simply restore the historic rights of Englishmen. The leading radical theorists however tended to abandon an appeal to history and stressed instead the natural and inalienable rights of all men. They rejected the arguments of veteran reformers such as John Cartwright and John Horne Tooke and built upon the earlier rational theories of John Locke and Richard Price who had asserted the natural rights of all men. Recognizing that the weight of historical evidence supported the conservative claim that there had always been a propertied franchise, these radical theorists preferred to claim those rights which all men *ought* to have because of their natural equality and common humanity. In the first volume of his *Rights of Man* (1791) Thomas Paine deliberately abandoned any appeal to the past and insisted that each age had the right to establish any political system which would fit its own needs. Paine contemptuously dismissed the much-vaunted Glorious Revolution and compared it unfavourably to the much more radical revolutions in America and France. The authority of the Revolution settlement in Britain, so forcibly defended by Edmund Burke, should only be accepted so long as the people regarded its terms as beneficial. The present age must be free to reject the tyranny of the past and to inaugurate a new age of more extensive liberty. Paine and other radical theorists insisted that all men were created equal and that they possessed inalienable natural rights which no government could legitimately infringe. These natural rights included the rights to life, liberty, property and the pursuit of happiness. To ensure that these natural rights were maintained in civil society, the authority of those in power must be limited and must be subject to the sovereignty of the people. A written constitution must place limits on the executive and the legislature, and must clearly delineate the civil rights of all subjects. It was essential that all men should possess an active voice in the decision-making processes of the state, so that the sovereign will of the people could exercise a vigilant and continuous super-vision over the actions of those in positions of power.

This emphasis on the equal political rights of all men led some radicals to go further than any of the earlier reformers and to condemn all hereditary honours, titles and privileges. Thomas Paine advocated the creation of a democratic republic, but few of the Jacobin societies went so far. They may well have agreed with Paine that there was no moral justification for hereditary legislators and no

14

rational grounds for dividing the nation into the separate interests of King, Lords and Commons, but they recognized that any overt attack on monarchy or aristocracy would alienate any support which they might hope for from the propertied elite. Nevertheless, it is clear that these societies believed that much of the misery in the world was produced by the pride, arrogance and ambition of kings and noblemen. It was a monstrous injustice to raise huge sums of money by taxing the poor in order to keep a few men in luxury. It was contrary to the evidence of nature to claim that strength, industry, intelligence, honesty or virtue were inherited qualities possessed only by the great landed families of Britain. Social, economic and political distinctions could be earned only by intrinsic personal merit and this could be found throughout all sections of society.

Despite their insistence that all men should enjoy equal political rights, it is not absolutely clear that the British Jacobins genuinely desired to live under a government of the people. Most of these radicals were men with a middle-class background or were drawn from the more respectable and skilled ranks of the working population. Few of them could entirely escape the assumption that men of property and education should govern and should give a lead to the labouring masses. James Mackintosh and John Thelwall, for example, expected the lower orders to follow the lead of enlightened men in the middle and upper ranks of society. Furthermore, in the struggle for the rights of man, most radicals were concerned quite literally with the liberty of adult males rather than with the freedom of all mankind. They regarded the position of women as analogous to that of children – they were dependent creatures, incapable of exercising independent political judgement. Even Mary Wollstonecraft, who was deeply concerned about the social and economic position of women, did not bother to campaign for votes for women. One or two radicals, most notably Thomas Spence, did imply that women too should be given the franchise, but the radical campaign was overwhelmingly preoccupied with securing the vote for adult males.

In the 1790s both radical theorists and radical societies were primarily concerned with campaigning for parliamentary reform. This emphasis is rather puzzling to later generations who have come to believe that the conditions of the poor can be improved only by economic reforms. The British Jacobins however had two strong motives for concentrating on parliamentary reform. They feared that any assault on private property would alienate the propertied elite and might provoke the poor into attacking the smaller possessions of the middling orders and the skilled tradesmen and artisans. More important was their conviction that many of the social and economic grievances of the poor were in fact created by the existing political system and could be removed by a radical reform of that system. It was the unequal distribution of political power, rather than the unequal distribution of wealth, that was the chief source of the economic grievances of the people. It was because a minority of rich landowners dominated the political system that government and Parliament neglected the interests of the rest of the population. The need to support an extravagant monarchy and aristocracy, the money lavished on corrupting the legislature and the enormous cost of foreign wars all combined to place a crippling tax burden on the middling and lower orders. Under the present corrupt system of government the majority of the population was impoverished in order to enrich the ruling minority. Economic inequality was natural and unavoidable, but the distinctions between rich and poor were grossly exaggerated by a political system designed to aid the few at the expense of the many. Parliamentary reform would produce a just government which would spend far less money on political corruption, on lavishing rewards on the privileged elite, and on wars of aggression. It would also abandon aggressive policies abroad and hence spend much less on its armed forces. The savings achieved in these ways would mean reduced taxes and more money left in the pocket of the ordinary subject.

For many radicals, political reform was an essential first step, to be followed by a series of other reforms passed by a legislature more responsive to the wishes of the people. Parliamentary reform would also lead to the abolition of tithes paid to the established church, to the repeal of the game laws, to reform of the laws which put so many debtors into prison, and so on. The address of the LCS to the inhabitants of Great Britain on 16 August 1792 claimed that the restoration of political liberty would see

> the press free, the laws simplified, judges unbiassed, juries independent, needless places and pensions retrenched, immoderate salaries reduced, the public better served, taxes diminished and the necessaries of life more within the reach of the poor, youth better educated, prisons less crowded, old age better provided for, and sumptuous Feasts, at the expense of the starving poor, less frequent. (Thale, 1983, p. 18)

The enormously successful and influential second volume of Paine's *Rights of Man* (1792) showed how a reformed government could alleviate the distress of the poor. Paine argued that a democratic government would reduce taxes on the poor but also levy a special property tax on the rich in order to raise enough money to relieve the condition of the poor. He proposed child allowances of £4 per annum for every child of a poor family until it reached the age of fourteen; old age pensions of £6 per annum for those over the age of fifty and £10 per annum for those over sixty; maternity allowances of £1 for each child born to a poor family; and a marriage grant of £1 to each poor couple. In a few remarkable pages Paine made one of the most original contributions to the whole reform programme.

Although the radicals hoped that parliamentary reform would lead to reduced taxes and some alleviation of economic distress, they specifically denied the charge that they were social and economic levellers who wished to confiscate private property and redistribute the wealth of the nation. The LCS and the Manchester radicals published handbills explicitly rejecting any suggestion that they wished to undermine the principle of private property or the rights of inheritance. The authors of the Manchester handbill were adamant:

> The equality insisted on by the friends of reform is AN EQUALITY OF RIGHTS. . . . The *inequality* derived from labour and successful enterprise, the result of superior industry and good fortune, is an *inequality essential to the very existence of Society*, and it naturally follows, that the property so acquired, should pass *from a father to his children*. To render property insecure would destroy all motives to exertion, and tear up public happiness by the roots.

Even the artisans of the Sheffield SCI claimed:

> we demand equality of rights, in which is included equality of representation. . . . We are not speaking of that visionary equality of property, the practical assertion of which would desolate the world, and replunge it into the darkest and wildest barbarism. (Dickinson, 1977, p. 255)

Even Thomas Paine feared social revolution and proposed to go no further than a tax on property to pay for his social welfare programme. John Thelwall wanted to improve the appalling conditions of the poor, but he believed that any attack on private property would produce complete anarchy and a more intolerable tyranny than any yet experienced. In his *Enquiry concerning Political Justice* (1793), William Godwin expressed the pious hope that the rich would voluntarily surrender their excess wealth to those who had most need of it. In his utopian world, wealth would go to those who most needed it. Godwin utterly opposed the idea of using violence or legislative action to deprive the wealthy of their property

17

Only Thomas Spence, in several of his publications, put forward a detailed Land Plan which would place the land and the natural resources of each parish under the control of parochial corporations made up of every man, woman and child resident in the parish. The land and resources would be rented out to the highest bidder and the income used on public amenities and on equal payments to every inhabitants of the parish (Dickinson, 1982; Dickinson, 1977, chapter 7).

Methods and Activities

The British Jacobins were committed to a radical reform of Parliament, but most of them were not republicans like Paine and few of them had worked out a programme of social and economic reforms. They were clearly uncertain about how best to improve the condition of the people. They were also uncertain and divided about what methods and tactics to adopt in order to achieve their aims. Nearly all of them favoured an appeal to reason and a propaganda campaign designed to expose the abuses of the present political system and to raise the political consciousness of the people. They found it difficult to agree on what policy should be pursued if rational persuasion failed to achieve their objectives. Only a minority considered any kind of physical force tactic which would apply irresistible pressure to the governing elite. Fewer still contemplated violent revolution, though this did find more adherents when government repression made it impossible to continue an open propaganda campaign for radical reform (see chapter 3).

The one area of substantial agreement among the radicals was the determination to educate the people about their political rights. Many optimistically believed that a propaganda campaign would be a sufficient means of accomplishing the reform of Parliament. A meeting of delegates from various radical societies, convened at Norwich on 24 March 1792, declared:

> We believe that instructing the people in political knowledge and in their natural and inherent rights as men is the only effectual way to obtain the grand object of reform, for men need only be made acquainted with the abuses of government and they will readily join in every lawful means to obtain redress. (Dickinson, 1977, p. 260)

All the radical societies organized meetings for political discussions and helped to disseminate printed political propaganda. Members attending the divisional meetings of the LCS for example spent much

18

of their time in listening to someone reading political literature or in taking part in political discussions. Debates were held in an orderly manner according to strict rules of conduct. There was to be no drunkenness, rowdiness or interruptions of speeches. All speakers were to address the chairman, no one was to speak for more than ten minutes at a time, and no one was to speak twice until everyone who wanted to speak had spoken once. The aim was clearly to promote the political education of the members while instilling in them both discipline and self-respect. The people must be taught to think for themselves as a prelude to acting for themselves. To propagate its views more widely, the LCS sold broadsheets and pamphlets, distributed large numbers of its own printed addresses, and tried to establish its own political magazine. It managed to publish an eight-page weekly, *The Politician*, four times betweeen December 1794 and January 1795, and a forty-eight page monthly, *The Moral and Political Magazine*, twelve times between June 1796 and May 1797. Both of these publications were collections of letters on political subjects, extracts from political speeches or lectures by radicals such as John Thelwall and John Horne Tooke, brief essays and selected passages from political classics. Unfortunately, the monthly magazine was a heavy financial drain on the resources of the LCS because they could only manage to sell half of its regular production of between 3,000 and 4,000 copies. As its name implies, the LCS also devoted a considerable amount of its time, effort and finances to correspondence with radical groups throughout the country, as well as with the French.

The radical societies in the provinces also held regular political debates and put a high premium on the production and dissemination of printed propaganda. In Manchester the radicals produced their own excellent weekly newspaper, the *Manchester Herald*, though this only flourished for a year – from March 1792 to March 1793 – before government prosecution closed it down. In Sheffield, Joseph Gales produced the *Sheffield Register* which circulated throughout the whole region; for a time he also produced a fortnightly periodical, *The Patriot*. From April 1792 to June 1794 *The Patriot* reported on radical developments in Britain and France, published editorials and letters, and quoted from all kinds of political literature. An excellent weekly periodical, *The Cabinet*, which published similar material, was produced in Norwich between 1794 and 1795. Elsewhere, Richard Phillips established the *Leicester Herald*, which lasted from May 1792 until November 1795; the radicals in Derby had the support of the *Derby Mercury*; those in Nottingham were aided by the *Newark Herald*; those in Cambridge by the *Cambridge Intelligencer*; while those on

Tyneside had the sympathetic assistance of Solomon Hodgson's *Newcastle Chronicle*.

A few radical theorists and publicists made heroic efforts to reach a mass audience with their political views. Some, such as John Thelwall and Henry Redhead Yorke, went on lecture tours, but most relied on printed literature. Daniel Isaac Eaton produced *Politics for the People*, a cheap (twopence per issue) weekly periodical that appeared between September 1793 and January 1795. Thomas Spence's *Pig's Meat* – the cheapest of all radical periodicals at one penny per issue – appeared between 1793 and 1795. Thelwall's *The Tribune* was published weekly from March 1794 to April 1795. Anxious to reach a mass audience, these men ransacked reform literature of the past two centuries in order to instruct the people in their political rights, and they disseminated this information in a cheap and easily digested form. Many other radicals produced an impressive array of individual pamphlets, but none could match the success of Paine's *Rights of Man* (1791–2). Published in many cheap editions it reached tens of thousands, perhaps hundreds of thousands, of readers. This enormous success owed much to the appeal of Paine's radical views, especially his ideas for relieving the distress of the labouring poor, but it was also due to Paine's ability to communicate with ordinary men. Paine was very conscious of his audience and of the effect that he wished to have on his readers. His style was bold and clear, his case was well-ordered and carefully marshalled, and he had a rare gift for combining lucid, rational argument with the capacity to touch the heart and stir the imagination. Paine's work was not as philosophically profound as William Godwin's *Enquiry concerning Political Justice* (which had a very considerable influence on radical intellectuals), but in his ability to reach a mass audience Paine stood head and shoulders above all other radical theorists.

Political education was the primary function of the radical societies of the 1790s, but there was also some recognition of the need for displays of unity and for demonstrations of mass support that would exert pressure on the governing elite. Efforts were made to promote joint activities by the various radical societies. There was some attempt to co-ordinate petitions in favour of Charles Grey's motion for parliamentary reform in 1793, but this did not match the earlier petitioning campaigns of the Wilkites and the Association movement. There was no nationwide petitioning campaign, only a rash of separate petitions which failed to demonstrate overwhelming support for the radical cause. Thirty-six petitions were sent to the House of Commons, but twenty-four of these were from Scotland,

20

and not one was from an English county. The Sheffield petition attracted about 8,000 signatures; that from London could secure only 6,000 signatures; while the petition from Norwich was signed by. no more than 3,700 people (Goodwin, 1979, pp. 277–80). These certainly indicated that there was a considerable body of people desiring parliamentary reform, but they failed to demonstrate anything like mass support or an irresistible tide in favour of change. The radicals were more successful in 1795 when, allied with the Foxite opposition in Parliament and moderate opinion out-of-doors, they organized a nationwide protest against the Government's repressive legislation. On this issue some ninety-five petitions, with over 130,000 signatures, were presented to Parliament. In defence of the traditional liberties of free speech and free assembly the radicals could rally an impressive degree of support, but even this effort failed in this instance to prevent the legislation reaching the statute book.

Some radicals were prepared to go much further than the employment of the well-established technique of persuasion and petitioning. They took up the idea of calling a National Convention, a proposal first suggested by James Burgh in 1774, and subsequently advocated by Thomas Paine and Joseph Gerrald. These theorists had suggested that a National Convention could emulate the American and French efforts to draw up a written constitution and to challenge the established political institutions of the state. Few radical activists were prepared to take such a revolutionary step, but they did favour a Convention which would unite the various radical societies behind an agreed reform programme that could be presented to Parliament and the people. The first practical steps towards a National Convention were taken by the Scottish reformers in December 1792 when some 160 delegates representing eighty radical societies in Scotland met in Edinburgh. They agreed on resolutions in support of moderate parliamentary reform, though the two leading delegates, Thomas Muir and William Skirving, held more advanced views. Muir read what some regarded as a seditious address from the United Irishmen in Dublin, and the Convention's adjournment was marked by French revolutionary procedures including the Jacobin oath to 'live free or die'. When the Convention reassembled in Edinburgh on 30 April 1793 it was again divided between moderates and radicals, though the latter secured a resolution in favour of inviting English delegates to a larger Convention in the autumn. Before that could meet, Thomas Muir was found guilty of sedition and sentenced to transportation to Botany Bay.

The unjust and vindictive trial of Muir provoked widespread

indignation and failed to divert some of the English radical societies from sending delegates to Edinburgh. The LCS sent Maurice Margarot and Joseph Gerrald and the London SCI sent Charles Sinclair and Henry Redhead Yorke. Margarot also represented the Norwich radicals, and the Sheffield SCI finally selected a delegate of their own. Although only a few English delegates managed to attend the National Convention in Edinburgh, their reputation and experience enabled them to play a decisive role in the assembly's deliberations. They devised its regulations, presided over its meetings and initiated its policies. Their commitment to radical parliamentary reform, their adoption of French revolutionary procedures and their uncompromising defiance of established authority impressed the Scottish radicals but alarmed those in power. The Convention started its meetings on 19 November 1793, but its brave show of resistance to oppression and its expressions of solidarity failed to prevent the Scottish authorities closing its proceedings on 5 and 6 December. Though the Convention had never advocated violence several of its leading members, including Skirving, Margarot and Gerrald, were convicted of sedition and transported to Botany Bay. The idea of a National Convention was a significant innovation, but the radicals had seriously miscalculated the extent of popular support for its activities and they had dangerously underestimated the fears which it would arouse among those in authority (Goodwin, 1979, pp. 284–306).

The most obvious weakness of radical strategy in the 1790s was the failure to rally the labouring poor to the cause of parliamentary reform. Very few radicals showed any appreciation of organized labour, nor did they seek to capitalize on the popular tradition of riots and crowd demonstrations as a means of putting pressure on the governing elite, or contemplate violent revolution on the French model. The leadership of the radical movement was dominated by men from the middling ranks of society. Such men had little direct contact with workers' combinations and they were fearful of alienating men of property by appearing to condone violent or direct action. Their overriding concern was to secure political equality, not to alleviate the economic conditions of the poor.

Although trade unions had begun to appear in a number of industries, and had already demonstrated their strength in a number of violent disorders and effective strikes, most radicals had not yet grasped that labour's industrial strength might be a powerful weapon of political change. Most radical theorists were still limited by their bourgeois conceptions of society and still concentrated on the freedom of the individual. There are some indications that a few radicals were groping towards a recognition of the value of organized workers and a concept of the theory of labour. Both John Thelwall and Thomas Paine complained that rich employers were able to combine to fix the wages and conditions of their employees, but that the authorities opposed efforts by the workers to unite in defence of their economic interests by organizing the peaceful withdrawal of their labour. Thelwall and William Godwin recognized the important role of labour in the production of wealth, but they did not develop this insight into a coherent theory of labour which might have enabled them to argue more effectively for a fairer redistribution of wealth. Thelwall also dimly perceived that the working conditions of the poor, which brought them together for a large part of the day, might provide them with a greater awareness of their grievances and a better opportunity to combine their numerical strength. This idea did not, however, lead Thelwall to suggest that the workers might be the means of their own salvation if they put their numerical strength and economic value to good use. None of the radicals advocated economic action, through the industrial strike for example, as a means of wringing substantial concessions from the propertied classes. Few radicals sprang from the ranks of the poor or fully identified with the labouring masses. In the realm of practical affairs there was some overlap between those who were members of radical societies and those who were involved in trade union activity, but this did not lead to the idea that the trade unions should be harnessed to the cause of parliamentary reform. There were also isolated examples of political slogans being used during industrial disputes and food riots, as on Tyneside in 1792–3 and Sheffield in 1795, but these riots and strikes were not primarily concerned with political issues and very few of those involved were political radicals (McCord, 1968; Wells, 1977a).

From 1795, when the radical societies were faced with government repression, there were signs that the political activists were beginning to appreciate the value of crowd demonstrations, but there was no strategy of using widespread rioting as a means of influencing the ruling oligarchy. The radicals had occasionally held public dinners or open-air meetings which had attracted over one thousand people, but it was not until 1795 that the LCS began to hold monster meetings to demonstrate the mass support which it could rally to the cause of reform. On 26 October 1795, a vast crowd, reputed to be 100,000 strong, assembled in the fields near Copenhagen House to hear speeches in favour of political reform and peace with France from John Thelwall, John Gale Jones and John Binns. This meeting provoked government repression in the form of the Seditious

Meetings Act and the Treasonable Practices Act, but before these measures were passed the radicals had held similar meetings. On 12 November 1795, a larger crowd, perhaps the greatest gathering yet assembled for a political cause, again met near Copenhagen House to hear John Thelwall, John Ashley and Richard Hodgson condemn the Government's policies. A similar protest meeting was held in Marylebone Fields on 7 December. These crowds demonstrated mass opposition to the Government's repressive policies, and there were also protests against the high price of food and the enormous costs of the war. It is unlikely that all those present supported a radical reform of Parliament, but those meetings were a significant innovation in radical strategy. They did not indicate though, as the authorities feared, that the radicals planned to move from peaceful crowd demonstrations to violent riots. Some radicals did try to whip up food rioters in Sheffield in 1795 to protest against the war with France and to demand parliamentary reform, and similar tactics were adopted during some food riots in the north west of England in 1800, but these were isolated examples and were not part of any general strategy by the political radicals (Goodwin, 1979, pp. 391–8).

The British Jacobins used many of the same tactics as earlier reformers in their attempts to achieve political change. They did develop some new approaches to the daunting task of applying pressure to an entrenched and confident propertied elite, but they failed to exploit the strength of the organized sections of the labour force and they were reluctant to provoke a wave of industrial disorder or violent riots. When the governing classes refused to concede reform, resorting instead to repression and persecution, most radicals lost heart or at least moderated their public conduct. As a last resort, however, a minority turned to conspiracy and violence. Most radicals had always denied that they wished to initiate a violent revolution in Britain and there is no reason to doubt their word. Faced with government repression in the later 1790s, an alienated remnant of the British Jacobins did assume the conspiratorial, treasonable and violent character which its earlier leaders had vigorously repudiated. Their activities will be explored in chapter 3, but first we must understand why the peaceful campaign for reform failed to achieve its objectives, and how the forces of conservatism drove some radicals towards revolution.

2 Conservative Reaction and Government Repression

Historians who have written on the radical movement of the 1790s have often been so captivated by the noble and heroic efforts of the reformers that they have tended to exaggerate the strength and unity of those who desired political change. They have not always recognized that the radicals agreed on very little except the need for a more equal representation of the people, that they never developed the organization or tactics capable of bringing irresistible pressure to bear upon the governing classes, and that they failed to rally the vast majority of the labouring poor behind their reform programme. The radicals attracted their greatest support when economic distress acted as a recruiting agent. Ultimate success had to await the further development of industrialization and urbanization that would transform the whole economy and social structure of Britain. In misjudging the strength of the radicals in the 1790s, sympathetic historians have had to explain their failure by concentrating on the panic reaction of the propertied classes to the excesses of the French Revolution, and the determination of the Government to suppress any radical threat at home. This is only a partial explanation for the collapse of the radical cause. The governing classes certainly adopted a policy of vigorous repression to cripple the reform movement, but the radicals did not simply capitulate to the application of greater force. The opponents of reform also developed an intellectual and moral defence of the existing political and social order that carried conviction, not only with the propertied elite, but also with large sections of the British people. The triumph of this conservative reaction was as much a propaganda victory as a success for the forces of law and order.

Ideology and Propaganda

The bulk of the propertied classes in Britain did not need the French Revolution or even the sophisticated arguments of Edmund Burke's

Reflections on the Revolution in France (1790) to teach them to fear radical reform or to fight to preserve the existing social order. Events in France certainly heightened their perception of what was at stake, though they were rather slower than Burke in recognizing that the Revolution was a threat to the traditional political and social order throughout Europe; but a steady belief in the virtues of the British constitution and a firm resistance to change were apparent long before the 1790s. Developments in France and at home, however, brought to light attitudes which had long existed under the surface: an almost unthinking acceptance of the existing constitution, an instinctive fear of change, and the conviction that power could only be entrusted to the propertied elite. Once these assumptions came under challenge from radicals at home and revolutionaries abroad, the defenders of the prevailing order were quick to develop a conservative ideology of considerable appeal, endurance and intellectual power. The first objective in the conservative reaction to the radical threat was to persuade the public in general, and the governing elite in particular, that the reforms suggested by the British Jacobins would destroy the established political and social order as the revolutionaries in France had done. The anarchy in France was therefore contrasted with the stability and prosperity of Britain. The second objective of the conservatives was to mount an attack on the intellectual foundations of the radical case and to articulate an ideology which would provide a strong buttress to the existing order. The overall strategy was to prove that the radicals were not fit to govern and that those in power in Britain under the present constitution happened to be those who ought to exercise authority in a well-constituted state.

Numerous conservative publications exploited such events in France as the September Massacres and the execution of Louis XVI and Marie Antoinette in order to demonstrate in vivid and gory detail the horrors of revolution and social anarchy. The French Revolution was shown to inflict great hardship on the poor, as well as destroying established order, hierarchy and justice. The radicals within Britain were also portrayed as dangerous demagogues and ambitious malcontents, jealous of the deserved honours and privileges of the ruling oligarchy. The only Britons who would be seduced by the Jacobin radicals were the idle and the dissolute, the thieves, cheats and propertyless beggars of society. The aims of the British Jacobins were deliberately misrepresented and the consequences of adopting their ideals were grossly exaggerated. Parliamentary reform was portrayed as the first step towards the destruction of monarchy and aristocracy. Attacks on political privileges were seen as a prelude to an assault on private property and all social distinctions. In a wild effort to make all men equal the rich would be plundered and the poor would be utterly ruined. Only idle demagogues could profit from the confusion produced by revolution. In contrast to the horrors already produced by revolution abroad and threatened by radicalism at home, conservative propagandists depicted Britain as the most prosperous country on earth, with her subjects enjoying life, liberty and property under a system of equal justice and the rule of law. True liberty, it was claimed, rested on the security of life and property. In Britain both rich and poor stood equal before the law and secure in the possession of their goods. The industrious poor were preserved and protected by a propertied elite who took their duties seriously.

This kind of propaganda appealed at a simple emotional level to a deep hatred of the French and a profound fear of radical change, but a more sophisticated intellectual response to the demand for reform was developed in the 1790s. Conservative theorists claimed that the British constitution secured the benefits of liberty, stability and prosperity because it was a mixed government which combined the virtues of monarchy, aristocracy and democracy through the institutions of King, Lords and Commons. Any attack on monarchy or aristocracy would result in a dangerously unstable democracy in which all subordination would be destroyed and the voice of reason would be drowned by the clamour of violence and enthusiasm. To avoid anarchy it was essential that King and Lords should deploy their patronage in order to influence the composition of the House of Commons and so cement the three parts of the legislature into a harmonious whole. The twin benefits of liberty and stability could only be secured while property could exercise its natural influence. Men of property deserved to be represented in Parliament because they contributed so much to the wealth of the country, and because they could be trusted to exercise the vote with a due regard to their own interests and those of the nation at large. The possession of property attached a man to his country and gave him an interest which he would always strive to protect. In contrast, those without property had no firm interest to protect and were not independent of the will of others. The poor were ill-informed, too ready to defer to their immediate superiors and too easily deluded and inflamed by unstable demagogues. It was therefore quite legitimate to deny such men the vote. The existing electoral system, despite its apparent irregularities and even its absurdities, produced a House of Commons which represented the powerful and legitimate social and economic interests in the country. Men of the greatest wealth, highest status and most eminent talents were chosen to represent the people. Since the best men sat in Parliament it mattered little how they were elected.

Conservative propaganda was not content merely to demonstrate the practical benefits of the existing political system or to show how these were achieved. It also sought to destroy the moral and intellectual foundations of the radical appeal to the doctrine of natural rights. Conservative theorists rejected the notion of natural equality and opposed the claim that all men should possess the right to vote. They also denied that civil governments were created solely to convert man's inalienable natural rights into extensive civil liberties or that those in authority should follow the dictates of pure reason.

While they admitted that all men possessed a common humanity, conservatives argued that men were so unequal in body, mind and fortune that they could not lay claim to an equal share of power in the state. Only a minority of men possessed solid judgement, ample intelligence and the ability to command others. These qualities were most likely to be found among men of birth and fortune who enjoyed the independence, leisure and education needed to prepare a man for the task of governing others. It was natural and inevitable therefore that this gifted minority should exercise the greatest power in the state and that inferior men should submit to their superiors. Violence would be needed to destroy the natural hierarchy in society and to enforce an unnatural equality. All men possessed the right to justice and to the legal protection of their life, personal liberty and private property, but they did not have a natural right to exercise political power in the state or to vote for members of the legislature. Power of this kind was not a natural right belonging to all men, but a legal right which any civil government was free to confer or deny as it saw fit. It was not a natural right because it could not be defended either as a necessary means of preserving civil government or as essential to the protection of the subject. It was a matter of expedience and prudence to decide who could be safely trusted with such power, and each society must reach its own decision on the issue. It was therefore legitimate for Britain to grant the vote to the propertied minority.

While the radicals insisted that civil government was created to convert man's natural rights into extensive civil liberties, conservative theorists maintained that government was necessary to protect private property, to preserve the natural distinctions in society and to restrain man's selfish and passionate nature. The most stable governments were the product of the needs and fears of men, not the deliberate result of reason or will. Their authority did not rest on any original contract or on known first principles, but on the history and experience of a particular society. The British constitution was prescriptive in that it had existed time out of mind and was the fruit of experience and the result of trial and error over centuries. It had made thousands of adjustments to the needs created by altered circumstances and the changing habits of the people. Human experience was more important than human reason in judging the merits of such a constitution. It was dangerously conceited for even the wisest and shrewdest of men to presume to elevate their reason above the judgement of centuries. A reverence for the past and an acceptance of the authority of the actual laws of a society were to be admired more than efforts to create a new order on the basis of speculative theories or attempts to ground authority on appeals to abstract general principles. The state was a complex organism that could not be easily remodelled and ought not to be lightly altered. Abstract rational principles were an inadequate guide to political action. It was a primary dictate of prudence not to prefer pure reason above the rooted opinions, traditions and prejudices of society (Dickinson, 1977, pp. 270–318).

Both the exaggerated hostility to the French Revolution and the sophisticated attack on the intellectual claims of the British radicals first appeared in Edmund Burke's *Reflections on the Revolution in France* in November 1790. While many of the propertied elite were still prepared to reserve judgement on the French Revolution, Burke was determined to alert the country to the dangers which he perceived. Horrified by developments in France he was also quite terrified at the possibility of similar changes within Britain. Much of his work was a denunciation of Richard Price and other radicals who desired parliamentary reform. If they were not opposed these reformers would destroy the established order in church and state, eliminate hierarchy, harmony and justice, and encourage the impoverished masses to pillage the wealth of the rich. Burke's fears did not find immediate acceptance, but, as anarchy, terror and war advanced in France, and as the British Jacobins gained in strength at home, his alarm call was increasingly heeded. Hatred of the French revolutionaries and fear of what the British radicals might do came to dominate a major propaganda campaign waged in Parliament and the press. A growing number of politicians began to follow Burke's lead and to reiterate his arguments. The Government's support in Parliament steadily grew as the more conservative Whigs followed Burke's example and broke away from Charles James Fox and the more liberal Whigs. The parliamentary support for even very moderate reform was reduced to a tiny rump of fifty or so MPs.

Burke's fears, though not necessarily all of his specific arguments, began to influence a veritable flood of conservative literature. Among the more sophisticated and influential works were John Bowles, *A Protest against T. Paine's Rights of Man* (1792), William Playfair, *Inevitable Consequences of a Reform in Parliament* (1792), William Vincent, *Short Hints upon Levelling* (1792), Robert Nares, *Principles of Government* (1792), Arthur Young, *The Example of France, A Warning to Britain* (1793), John Reeves, *Thoughts on English Government* (1795), and the sermons of such conservative clerics as Samuel Horsley, William Paley and Richard Watson. Some of these works were circulated among the lower orders by the Loyalist organizations which sprang up in response to the rise of the British Jacobins. These organizations also aped the radical publications of Daniel Eaton and Thomas Spence. They produced cheap conservative tracts based on collections of essays, letters, speeches, poems and extracts from political classics. Counter-revolutionary propaganda of a more sophisticated kind appeared in *The Anti-Jacobin*, a weekly magazine organized by George Canning, William Gifford and John Hookman from November 1797 to July 1798. With occasional contributions from leading politicians this miscellany sold about 2,500 copies each week and the collected work later went through four editions. It was succeeded by the *Anti-Jacobin Review and Magazine*, a monthly which flourished until 1821. Even more successful in reaching the lower orders with conservative political propaganda was Hannah More. Encouraged by the Bishop of London she first produced the highly successful *Village Politics* in 1792 and then between 1795 and 1798 she produced a whole series of such pamphlets in her *Cheap Repository Tracts*. Nearly half of these tracts were written by Hannah More herself and the rest were contributed by those with similar views and the same purpose. By 1798 nearly two million copies had been sold at a penny or halfpenny each. They circulated widely in workplaces, schools, workhouses and even among the armed forces. Although many of the purchasers were men of property seeking to inculcate conservative values among the lower orders there can be no denying that they reached a much greater readership than the works of Paine or any other radical propagandist (Hole, 1983, pp. 53–69).

Political caricatures and cartoons were another way of reaching the lower orders, as well as the more educated public, with conservative propaganda. A great many caricaturists, including Isaac Cruickshank, James Gillray and Thomas Rowlandson, evidently admired the British constitution and wished to preserve it against assault from without and subversion from within. In numerous prints Paine, Price and Priestley were portrayed as dangerous conspirators plotting to destroy the constitution in church and state by violent means. The Revolution Society was criticized for drinking toasts against the King, the Norwich radicals were condemned for their readiness to sacrifice their country to French interests, while the London Corresponding Society was represented as a gang of brutal and impoverished conspirators. Many prints warned the nation of the horrors which would befall it should its cherished constitution ever be exchanged for the French model. Violence, tyranny and poverty would be the inevitable results. Some of these prints were subsidized by Loyalist associations so that they could be purchased more cheaply in bulk for distribution to the lower orders.

Many items in the conservative propaganda campaign were written by the political elite or produced directly at their instigation. This was not always the case as an investigation of the newspaper press clearly shows. Some of the leading London newspapers were controlled or subsidized by the propertied elite. Conservative propaganda could be expected in such obviously pro-government newspapers as the *Sun*, the *True Briton*, and the *Oracle*. In the provinces, however, the local newspapers were owned by independent middle-class proprietors. Many of these evidently held conservative views and recognized that most of their readers did too. Historians have tended to highlight the rise of the radical press in the provinces, but many newspapers poured out a steady stream of news and views designed to reinforce the status quo. The conservative *Manchester Mercury* and *Manchester Chronicle* sold at least as well and lasted longer than the radical *Manchester Herald*. On Tyneside the reforming publisher of the *Newcastle Chronicle* faced stiff competition from the conservative *Newcastle Advertiser* and *Newcastle Courant*. The *Courant* in particular regularly censured those who maliciously undermined the Government and frequently reported news which sought to damage the radical cause. With the issue of 14 May 1794, every reader of the *Courant* received a four-page pamphlet, *The Poor Man's Friend*, which warned the lower orders not to be led into sedition and disorder by ambitious fanatics. Conservative newspapers also worked hard to combat radical rivals in Leicester and Birmingham, even in Norwich and Sheffield. They easily carried the day in less industrialized regions, as can be seen by a perusal of such newspapers as the *York Courant*, the *Chelmsford Chronicle*, and the *Sussex Weekly Advertiser*.

31

Extra-parliamentary associations with a political objective are often regarded as the distinctive achievement of the radicals of the later eighteenth century. In fact, effective, widespread and popular organizations of this kind were also established by those who were opposed to change and who wished to thwart the aims of the reformers. During the 1790s several conservative or loyalist associations flourished in Britain. These were not simply the creation of the propertied elite foisted upon an unresponsive public. They appealed to many in the middle and lower ranks of society across the whole country. A desire to defend the status quo was the natural reaction of many ordinary people who were well aware of the considerable improvements made in Britain over the last century and who contrasted these with the recent breakdown of law and order in France.

The first signs of a conservative organization opposed to reform appeared in response to the Dissenters' campaign to repeal the Test and Corporation Acts between 1787 and 1790. This pressure alarmed the Anglican clergy who raised the old cry of 'the Church in danger' in order to rally opinion against repeal. During the debate on the issue, in March 1790, Edmund Burke rose to attack the whole doctrine of natural rights to which the Dissenters were appealing. He condemned Rational Dissenters such as Richard Price as atheists and anarchists whose subversive design was to undermine the established order in church and state. Burke's intervention in the debate was very effective, but more significant was the propaganda emanating from Church and King clubs which were founded in many parts of the country. These clubs were quite prepared to resort to intimidatory tactics in order to defeat the alliance of Dissenters and reformers. In Birmingham three local magistrates prompted and directed a popular demonstration against the Dissenters and reformers when they were celebrating Bastille day in July 1791. This demonstration of loyalty to Church and King soon degenerated into a violent riot which the magistrates failed to control. The meeting houses of the Dissenters were destroyed and the house of Joseph Priestley, the veteran reformer, was sacked. He and several other Dissenters were driven from the town and the reform movement was seriously weakened. Although the local Anglican magistrates protected many of the rioters it seems clear that conservative attitudes were quite popular in Birmingham (Rose, 1960). In Manchester, a Church and King club opposed any repeal of the Test and Corporation Acts and viewed with alarm the creation of radical societies dedicated to parliamentary reform. Its members accused the local radicals of conspiring to subvert the constitution, and they condemned the wild theories and seditious doctrines of those who threatened to bring confusion and anarchy to Britain. In December 1792 a Church and King mob directed its fears and hatred against the lives and property of prominent reformers in Manchester. There is evidence to suggest that the local magistrates gave tacit approval, perhaps even active encouragement to the rioters, but there are also clear signs of popular hostility to the reformers.

The Manchester riot was part of a much wider campaign, in late 1792, to rally conservative and loyalist opinion against the radicals. Events in France increased the Government's fear of reform at home and persuaded it to issue a royal proclamation on 21 May 1792 against seditious writings. Meetings in support of this proclamation were held in many parts of the country and were widely reported in the newspapers. In a determined effort to rally public opinion behind the existing constitution, local gentlemen, magistrates and Anglican clergymen across the country encouraged the drafting of some 386 loyal addresses to the King by September 1792. Impressed by this display of public support, the Government began to consider how best to exploit conservative opinion in the country in order to overawe the radicals. On 23 November 1792 a public announcement in the *Star*, a pro-government evening newspaper, urged the founding of an Association for the Preservation of Liberty and Property against Republicans and Levellers (APLP). The advertisement was placed by John Reeves, who later claimed to be acting independently, but who was a former chief justice of Newfoundland and acted as the Government's paymaster of the Westminster police judges. If he was not directly encouraged by the Government at least he knew that the scheme would meet with ministerial approval. The Government certainly welcomed the proposal and helped to publicize it.

The first APLP was set up by Reeves at the Crown and Anchor tavern in London in November 1792. By December several others had been founded in the metropolis and the neighbouring counties. Early in 1793 the association spread first to the West, then to the Midlands and finally to the North and East. Although rather weak in Norfolk and Lincoln, and probably non-existent in Northumberland, Cumberland and Westmorland, the APLP soon became the largest political organization in the country. The total number of associations certainly ran into the hundreds and may have been as high as the 2,000 which Reeves claimed. Active membership was largely confined to local men of property, though they were able to enlist considerable support from more humble men. In the rural areas the gentry, yeomanry and clergy played a prominent role in the committees of these loyalist associations, whereas in urban areas the activists were mainly merchants, manufacturers and professional men. In Manchester, for example, 37 per cent of members were manufacturers and 14 per cent were merchants, while in Birmingham a third were clergymen. The lower orders were not among the activists, but they must have been encouraged to support loyalist addresses. Dozens of loyalist addresses were signed by hundreds of local people, several were signed by over a thousand, while that from Bath was supported by an impressive 5,033 local inhabitants. It seems likely that these loyalist associations were more numerous and possibly more popular than the radical societies.

These loyalist associations adopted the organization and some of the tactics of the radical societies. Each association appointed a chairman, a secretary and a treasurer. Subscriptions were raised; discussions, dinners and processions were held; addresses and resolutions were passed; and the associations engaged in correspondence with each other. They also produced and disseminated a great deal of printed propaganda. Reeves's own London association produced much the best political literature. It published its own pamphlets and it distributed hundreds of conservative tracts including works by Hannah More, William Paley and John Bowles. The Manchester association was almost as active. It distributed 10,000 copies of its own conservative declaration in a mere two months, and 6,000 copies of other pamphlets. Nearly all of the loyalist tracts highlighted the political anarchy into which France had been plunged and contrasted this disastrous situation with the many benefits enjoyed by those living under the British constitution. The British radicals were accused of being the tools or dupes of the French and the people of Britain were advised to rally in defence of the existing social order (Dozier, 1983, pp. 53–69, 76–97; Mitchell, 1961; Ginter, 1966).

The loyalist associations were not content to rely upon persuasion, but resorted to intimidation and persecution in order to defeat their radical opponents. In Manchester the loyalist association, based on the revived Church and King club, encouraged the riot of December 1792 which resulted in a mob attacking the house of Thomas Walker and the offices of the *Manchester Herald*. There were several other riots in Manchester, Liverpool, Salford and other parts of south Lancashire in 1792–5. The crowds involved were often too large to be bands of hired ruffians (Booth, 1983). In many other parts of the country the loyalists organized banquets, processions, bonfires and other demonstrations of public support in order to intimidate their radical opponents. Thomas Paine was burned in effigy in dozens of towns across the country in late 1792 and early 1793. Many loyalist associations warned innkeepers and publicans that they might lose their licences if they allowed seditious meetings on their premises. Without access to these public rooms it was very difficult for the radicals to hold large or regular meetings. Many innkeepers and publicans were cowed by such threats. At Bath, on 20 December 1792, some 111 innkeepers and victuallers vowed not to allow meetings which would threaten to disturb the public peace. Nearly 700 signed a similar declaration in Sussex, and the example was followed in other towns. Many loyalist associations were also active in scrutinizing the activities of local radicals and in reporting any suspicious behaviour to the authorities. In many areas they acted as the eyes and ears of the Government; sometimes they even offered rewards to anyone who could provide proof of seditious activity.

Many loyalist associations had a short life because they soon destroyed the radical forces in their area. As the threat of internal revolution waned the loyalist propaganda effort weakened and the activities of the associations lost focus and direction. On the other hand, as the dangers of French invasion increased in 1793–5, some loyalist associations turned their attention to assisting the war effort. They increasingly joined forces with those whose prime aim was to defend the country and to win the war against France. The loyalist associations helped to raise bounties to assist in the recruitment of seamen, collected funds to relieve the dependents of men killed in the war, and purchased extra clothing and supplies for the army in Flanders. Tens of thousands of pounds were collected for these purposes in London, Portsmouth, Southampton, Newcastle, Manchester and many other towns. As the war expanded and the threat of invasion grew, the loyalist associations even became a source of recruitment for an armed defence force designed to resist any invasion should it occur and to intimidate any surviving radicals at home.

The war with France stretched the manpower resources of the Government to the limit as it sought to expand the navy and the army as rapidly as possible. As a defence force against foreign invaders and as a police force to maintain internal order, the Government turned increasingly to the local county militias. These forces were denuded of troops, however, as the Government enticed the best men into the regular army; in addition to this, popular resistance built up in some areas against being balloted for service in the militia and then being used to suppress riots and industrial disorder. Clearly a larger and more dependable defence force was required to meet both external and internal threats of subversion. This recognition led to various suggestions for a paramilitary volunteer defence force which would arm the propertied classes while disarming the unreliable poor. These proposals were put to the Government and by February 1794 the cabinet was exploring the possibility of enlisting the gentry and yeomanry of the country into a cavalry defence force. In March 1794 the Government decided to raise such a force based on the loyalist organizations which were already in existence. It authorized the raising of the Volunteers. The elite cavalry units were to provide their own horses (which, of course, restricted the force to men of property), but the Government was to provide them and the infantry regiments with arms, uniforms and equipment. To pay for these the Government turned not to Parliament for public revenue, but appealed directly to loyalists to raise private subscriptions. Within weeks, seventeen counties and six towns had pledged nearly £100,000. Despite some opposition this money was raised from thousands of loyalists. The aristocracy and gentry made the largest contributions, but smaller sums were raised from many in the middling ranks of society. The largest sums were raised from such counties as Yorkshire and Wiltshire. In several towns, including London, Birmingham, Manchester, Exeter and Bradford, the loyalist associations raised their own Volunteer companies or transformed themselves bodily into Volunteer forces. In many other areas the loyalist associations provided much of the finance and many of the senior officers for the new defence force. Large numbers of men were raised before the end of 1794, but the Volunteer force continued to increase until it was about 450,000 strong when Britain faced invasion in 1804. Though never called upon to meet the French the Volunteers did become a major police force for the preservation of internal order. In many ways, however, its primary significance was as an instrument of propaganda. It demonstrated the willingness of the propertied classes to fight to preserve their privileged position. Only the totally reliable poor were allowed to join as private soldiers and even then they were commanded by their landlords and employers. The willingness to serve at any level became a political test of loyalty to the existing regime. The parades, the military exercises and the patriotic speeches at celebration dinners were all designed to demonstrate the strength and commitment of the propertied classes. The Volunteers not only sought to intimidate their radical opponents, they also succeeded in encouraging loyalty and patriotism among the public at large (Dozier, 1983, pp. 138–171; Western, 1956).

The royal proclamation against seditious writings of 21 May 1792 was the first step in the Government's campaign to exploit its executive, judicial and legislative powers in order to undermine and then destroy the radical movement within Britain. The Government's strategy has sometimes been termed 'Pitt's Reign of Terror', though the repression was less than that in contemporary France and pales in comparison with the policies of some modern regimes. Nonetheless, there can be no denying the Government's determination to destroy the radical threat or the suffering inflicted on many honest men whose only crime was a desire to improve the lot of the ordinary people.

Once the Government had convinced itself that the radicals posed a serious threat to law and order, the Home Office was instructed to investigate their activities and to scrutinize their writings. The Home Office comprised a Secretary of State (Henry Dundas until 1794 then the Duke of Portland), two permanent under-secretaries (the most active in the 1790s being Evan Nepean and John King), and a dozen or so clerks. In addition, from the Home Office Richard Ford supervised the London police office, which was established in 1792, and, from 1793, an Alien Office was set up under William Wickham as a sub-department of the Home Office with instructions to keep an eye on foreign visitors to Britain especially the French. A small secret service section was also created in which James Walsh was particularly active. The Home Office could call upon the assistance of the London police and stipendiary magistrates; it also collected information from the many sympathetic JPs and the hundreds of post office and customs officials spread across the whole country. JPs reported on any disorders, the Post Office opened the mail of suspected persons, and customs officials kept an eye on all travellers going in and out of the country. Diplomats abroad also sent in reports on the activities of British and Irish radicals who had left the country. Private individuals, including landowners and employers, clergymen and innkeepers, informed the Home Office of radical activity in their areas. Some of this information was clearly alarmist and exaggerated and some reports were motivated by spite, by a desire for revenge and by hopes of advancement. Evidence of this kind was often unreliable and biased, but the Home Office was not as naive or as gullible as its critics have maintained. It learned to sift the mass of reports and letters sent to it and it often showed a willingness to distrust its informants.

The Home Office has been most criticized for its use of spies and paid informers, some of whom built up successful careers as secret agents. Critics of these agents have accused them of fabricating evidence in order to advance their careers. They have even been condemned as agents provocateurs who deliberately misled foolish men into mouthing seditious words or engaging in subversive activity, before betraying them to the authorities. It seems likely that some spies acted in this way. James Powell was a government agent who actually joined the executive committee of the LCS in 1795 and later joined in the conspiracies of the United Englishmen. The reliability of government agents may have declined in the later 1790s, but, initially, the Home Office employed some very effective under-cover agents who successfully penetrated the LCS and other radical societies and who sent in detailed and reliable reports. George Lynam, William Metcalfe and John Groves all succeeded in masquerading as genuine radicals while supplying the Government with sober and accurate information. As the use of spies expanded, less efficient and less scrupulous men were sometimes employed, but the Home Office was not always taken in by the exaggerated reports of such unreliable agents as William Barlow. Since it sincerely believed that it was facing a subversive conspiracy, and by the late 1790s it was facing one, the Home Office had little alternative but to employ spies and informers (Emsley, 1979; Wells, 1983, chapter 2).

Government ministers genuinely believed that they faced a revolutionary conspiracy and were convinced that this danger justified stern action against the radicals. In their minds this threat merited the use of judicial and legislative powers. The most notorious examples of judicial prosecution were the trials for sedition in Scotland in 1793–4, and the treason trials in England in 1794. In Scotland, Thomas Muir and Thomas Fyshe Palmer were sentenced in 1793 to transportation to Botany Bay despite the absence of strong evidence against them. Hand-picked juries and a vindictive judge also secured the conviction of William Skirving Maurice Margarot and Joseph Gerrald in early 1794 for their activities in the National Convention at Edinburgh. Widespread indignation at these harsh sentences, and the brilliant legal skills of Thomas Erskine, helped to secure the acquittal of the leading English radicals when they were charged with treason in late 1794. Thomas Hardy, John Horne Tooke, Thomas Holcroft, John Thelwall and others were charged with high treason and every scrap of evidence was laid before the courts in an effort to convince the jury that the country had narrowly escaped violent revolution. Erskine was able to destroy the prosecution's case and to undermine the reliability and veracity of its key witnesses. After several acquittals had been welcomed by public rejoicing, the Government abandoned its attempts to secure convictions for high treason and released some of its other prisoners.

The Government had very little success in the other treason trials of the 1790s even when it was prosecuting men who were engaged in revolutionary conspiracies. In 1794 it did execute the leader of a plot to seize Edinburgh Castle, but, in 1798, after arresting many radicals who had close links with revolutionaries in France and Ireland, it was able to convict and execute only one of the conspirators, the Revd James Coigley (or O'Coigley). Others, including Arthur O'Connor and Colonel Despard, escaped conviction on this occasion, though they were almost certainly guilty of planning an insurrection. The Government was much more successful with the trials of those accused of publishing seditious libels or uttering seditious words. Many men were arrested for such offences though only about one case in three finally went to trial because it was recognized that it was difficult to provide conclusive evidence of such crimes, and juries were often unwilling to convict. In major cases the Government went to extraordinary lengths to secure a conviction. In some instances it resorted to ex-officio informations which allowed the Attorney General to avoid a preliminary hearing before a grand jury and enabled him to proceed directly to the trial of the accused. The accused was not always informed of the charges against him and there was no compulsion on the Attorney General to bring the case to trial. The threat of prosecution could be left hanging over the accused's head and, if he could not afford bail, he could technically be held in prison without trial. Daniel Isaac Eaton, Gilbert Wakefield and, later, William Cobbett all suffered under ex-officio informations and spent months in prison before any sentence was passed. In cases which were particularly complex the law also allowed the Attorney General to call for a special jury of men of a higher rank and superior education. Forty-eight names were put on a list of eligible jurors by the sheriff, but with the Crown Office's approval, and then the prosecution could scrutinize this list and delete as many as twelve names in order to weed out anyone who might be sympathetic to the accused. Even ordinary juries could be packed, as is indicated by the suspicious evidence of several men serving on the jury of more than one political trial in London in the 1790s. In some cases the authorities were prepared to use tainted or unreliable evidence in order to secure conviction. Thomas Walker, the leading Manchester radical, was undoubtedly framed on a conspiracy charge.

In trials involving charges of seditious libel, most of the accused were convicted. The total number of convictions in the 1790s, however, fell short of 200, and this hardly constitutes a government-inspired reign of terror. Nonetheless, many leading radicals were convicted on charges of seditious libel, including Daniel Isaac Eaton, Thomas Spence, John Thelwall, Gilbert Wakefield, Thomas Walker, Richard Phillips, the proprietor of the *Leicester Herald*, Daniel Holt of the *Newark Herald* and James Montgomery, the editor of the *Sheffield Iris*. Thomas Paine was convicted in his absence, while persecution and intimidation drove a number of eminent radicals into exile including Joseph Priestley, Joseph Gales, John Ashley, and Matthew Falkner and Samuel Birch who had published the *Manchester Herald*. Many of those who were found innocent had to spend time in prison awaiting trial, suffered loss of income and incurred the cost of their defence. Malicious prosecutions could bring severe hardship even if the ultimate verdicts resulted in acquittals. A few radicals, for example Thomas Spence, Arthur O'Connor, Colonel Despard, and John and Benjamin Binns, spent months in prison without even being convicted of an offence. The authorities may not have totally destroyed the rule of law in their efforts to destroy the radicals, as the many acquittals in political trials clearly testify, but they certainly bent and abused legal procedures and showed a ruthless determination to silence their critics.

In seeking to defeat the radicals, the Government may not have instituted a reign of terror, but ministers undoubtedly secured the support of Parliament for new legislation which would strengthen their hands in the campaign to crush all dangerous manifestations of dissent. To convince Parliament of the need for such repressive measures, the Government produced a mass of written material and a host of witnesses and informers before secret committees of the House of Commons in 1794 and 1799. The repressive legislation was bitterly denounced by liberal and radical opinion at the time – and has been condemned by many historians since – but, in fact, it was much less effective than has often been claimed. The suspension of habeas corpus, which allowed the Government to imprison subjects without trial, was a drastic infringement of the civil liberties of the subject, but the suspension only operated from May 1794 to July 1795 and from April 1798 to March 1801, and the authorities rarely exploited this particular means of silencing its opponents. Only a small number of radicals were imprisoned without being convicted of an offence. The infamous Two Acts of 1795 were also more significant as an indicator of government alarm and determination than as an effective weapon used to destroy the radicals. The Treasonable Practices Act of 1795 extended the law of treason in an alarming fashion to include anyone who, by speech or writing, 'compassed or devised' the death or deposition of the king or who sought either to force the king to change his ministers or to overawe Parliament. Despite the dangerously wide terms of this Act, which appeared to make outspoken criticism of the Government an act of treason, it was never in fact used and no radical was prosecuted under its provisions. The Sedition Meetings Act of 1795 also gave wide powers to magistrates over the holding of public meetings, but this legislation did not immediately stop the radical societies from operating. Indeed, the LCS actually increased its activities in the year following the passing of this Act. Only John Gale Jones was convicted under the Seditious Meetings Act, for a radical meeting held in Birmingham, though other radicals were acquitted or released before being brought to trial for offending against this measure.

Other repressive legislation was also less effective or less often implemented than has been thought. After the naval mutinies of 1797 a Bill was rushed through Parliament which made it a capital offence to encourage mutiny in the armed forces. There was only one prosecution under this Act, but even in this case the death sentence does not appear to have been invoked. In 1799 the leading radical societies were formally banned by law, but by then they were already in a state of collapse and the legislation was hardly necessary. In 1799, and more comprehensively in 1800, Parliament passed legislation making illegal all combinations of workers or trade unions. These organizations were regarded as conspiracies in restraint of trade. This measure was certainly a vindictive piece of class legislation which tried to weaken the ability of workers to improve their wages and conditions of work, but it did not in fact destroy all trade unions or make it impossible for workers to combine in industrial action. The Act of 1800 was rarely implemented, for even when employers sought to destroy the trade unions which had been formed by their workers they preferred to prosecute under the ordinary common law rather than under the terms of this particular measure (Emsley, 1981; Prochaska, 1973; M. Dorothy George, 1927–9).

Although the Government's repressive legislation was not often implemented the Acts passed were serious infringements of civil liberties and they were always a threat hanging over the heads of radicals and trade unionists. By the same token, although the Government did not arrest vast numbers of radicals, it did prosecute, harass and intimidate most of the leading radicals. These actions destroyed the effective leadership of the radical societies, silenced the most able radical propagandists, and frightened many of the rank

41

and file into abandoning the reform movement. Nonetheless, it can be seriously questioned whether judicial and legislative measures alone were responsible for the collapse of the radical movement in the later 1790s. The propertied classes mounted an extremely effective conservative propaganda campaign which convinced large sections of the population that the radicals were foolish innovators at best and dangerous traitors at worst. Internal disorder in France persuaded many British subjects to cherish the stability enjoyed under the British constitution, whereas war with France aroused a deep-seated patriotism more powerful and more widespread than any desire for political reform. There is little evidence to suggest that the radicals were ever in a position to capture the hearts and minds of the propertied classes or even of a majority of the labouring poor in the 1790s. It would be idle, however, to deny that a determined government made the task of the radicals quite impossible. The ruthlessness of the propertied elite caused suffering to many brave men who honestly endeavoured to improve the lot of their fellow citizens.

3 The Revolutionary Underground

The radical societies of the 1790s always explicitly renounced any desire to achieve their aims by force and even the leaders accused of treason in 1794 were acquitted of any charge of advocating violent revolution. Nearly all the radical theorists were cautious about suggesting the need for revolution. John Thelwall thought that a revolution might be provoked by a tyrannical government, but he always insisted that he himself wished to see a gradual transformation of society. William Godwin utterly rejected violence as a means of securing political reforms. Thomas Paine was more equivocal. He supported the idea of a national convention to establish a new constitution, but he never advised the people to take up arms. Both he and Thomas Spence appear to have envisaged a recourse to arms only after the governing classes had resorted to force to preserve their privileged position. Only James Oswald, in his *Review of the Constitution of Great Britain* (1793), appears to have been convinced that radical reforms could never be achieved by peaceful means. He maintained that only violent revolution could secure the rights of man, but he himself did not involve himself in violent action.

Despite the absence of any influential revolutionary ideology in the 1790s, and despite the express commitment of the radical societies to peaceful persuasion, the Government was convinced that a real threat of revolution existed. It brought forward a mass of evidence and a host of witnesses before the parliamentary committees of secrecy in 1794, 1799, 1801 and 1812, in an effort to prove its claims that an important element in the radical movement was dedicated to the violent overthrow of the state. It had little difficulty in convincing the conservative majority in Parliament of the existence of a revolutionary conspiracy, but many historians have had difficulty in accepting this evidence.

Some of this evidence was certainly gathered by local authorities who were easily alarmed by the slightest sign of political protest or social disorder. A lot of it was collected by spies and government agents who wished to ingratiate themselves with the ministers and who were not noted for their veracity or their reliability. Even those who tried to be objective had to rely heavily upon unsubstantiated rumours and second-hand accounts because revolutionary conspirators shunned publicity and operated in secrecy whenever possible. When more reliable evidence of revolutionary conspiracy is to hand, the historian still has to decide whether the plots were in any sense practical projects or merely the fantasies of deluded men, and whether they were the work of a tiny group of crack-brained fanatics or represented profound popular disenchantment with the prevailing social order. It is quite possible for the same evidence to be interpreted by historians in quite different ways. Much depends on the predispositions and the historical imagination of the historians concerned. Veitch (1913), Cannon (1973) and Thomis and Holt (1977) have tended to play down the significance of the threat of revolution in Britain, whereas Thompson (1968) and Wells (1983) have gone to considerable lengths to demonstrate how much support the revolutionaries possessed. Goodwin (1979) and Dinwiddy (1974, 1979) have accepted that a revolutionary movement existed, but they are less convinced of its effectiveness or its degree of popular support. It is unlikely that historians will ever reach full agreement on the issue, but to appreciate their difficulties it is necessary to examine the Irish revolutionaries, their contacts with and influence upon the various united societies in Britain, and the degree to which political objectives influenced the actions of those engaged in violent economic protests.

The Irish Revolutionaries

In the early 1790s a radical movement arose in Ireland that was very similar to those in England and Scotland in terms of origins, aims and even social composition. In Ireland a narrow oligarchy dominated the executive and used its patronage to influence the composition and decisions of the legislature. This oligarchy was in turn heavily influenced by the British Government which controlled appointments in the Irish administration. The vast majority of the population was denied any real influence in parliamentary elections or in the decision-making processes of the country. Political inequality was worse in Ireland, however, because of racial and religious discrimination. The Protestant Ascendancy, made up of rich, episcopalian and Anglo-Irish landlords, denied any significant political influence at national level to the Dissenters, chiefly of

44

Scottish descent, who lived mainly in Ulster, and opposed any kind of political representation to the Catholic native Irish who made up at least two-thirds of the population. Thus in Ireland, as in England, the demand for greater political liberty was bound up with the desire for greater religious freedom, but the barriers to change were very much higher.

As early as 1790 some Belfast Protestant radicals began to speak up in favour of parliamentary reform and an extension of the franchise to the Catholics. By the spring of 1791 Dr William Drennan, Theobald Wolfe Tone, Samuel Neilson and Thomas Russell were discussing the idea of setting up a Society of United Irishmen which would seek to unite Protestants and Catholics in a campaign for political and religious freedom. These Protestants believed that they could only succeed against the powerful and entrenched elite in Ireland if they could secure the support of the Catholic majority. To combat the strong Protestant distrust of the Catholics, Wolfe Tone produced *An argument on behalf of the Catholics of Ireland* (September 1791), which argued that the Catholics could be trusted with political power without this reform encouraging them to seek to recover the lands confiscated from them in the seventeenth century. At this stage, however, Tone wanted to restrict the Catholic franchise to £10 freeholders. For their part the Catholics were inclined to keep the Protestant radicals at arm's length. Their own representatives, who met together in Dublin as the General Committee of the Catholics, feared that the English Government which carried such influence over the Irish administration would resist concessions to the Catholics if they were seen to be too sympathetic to French revolutionaries or Irish radicals.

The first society of United Irishmen was established in Belfast in October 1791 by Tone, Drennan and Neilson. Most of its members were Protestants, though the society insisted that no reform of the system of representation was practicable or just which did not include Irishmen of every religious persuasion. A society set up in Dublin, a month later and with Napper Tandy as its secretary, had more success in attracting prominent Catholics to its ranks. By 1793 the Dublin society had a total membership of about 400, half of whom were quite regular attenders at meetings. There was almost an equal number of Protestants and Catholics, though the officers and leading activists were Protestants. About one quarter of the members were professional men, chiefly legal and medical men, and book-sellers or printers. There were as many merchants and manu-facturers, mainly engaged in the cloth trade, though the professional men held most of the offices in the Dublin society. Many of the other members were also drawn from the middle classes. There were a few craftsmen and artisans, but no significant support from the labouring poor. The society actually lost a considerable number of members when it finally came out in favour of universal manhood suffrage in 1794 (McDowell, 1940).

The United Irishmen found it very difficult to agree upon their political programme or to enlist the support of the Protestant and Catholic masses. The principle of universal manhood suffrage worried many Protestant reformers because the Catholics were such a clear majority in the country. Whereas the Catholics supported the idea of the secret ballot because they feared the influence which Protestant landlords could exert on their Catholic tenants and employees, many Protestants wanted to retain open voting precisely because of this. It was not until early 1794 that the United Irishmen finally published their radical programme. They came out for all the major radical demands for parliamentary reform, including universal manhood suffrage, but not the secret ballot. Many Catholics rightly feared that many Protestant reformers were not wholehearted supporters of complete equality between Protestants and Catholics. Their leaders still put faith in the Catholic Committee while many of the Catholic peasantry turned to the Defenders, a secret Catholic organization pledged to redress social, economic and religious grievances. Militant Protestants in Ulster set up rival sectarian organizations, including, from September 1795, the Orange Order. The United Irishmen strove valiantly to bridge this bitter divide, with only limited success. Sectarian violence blighted the lives of many in Ireland, especially in Ulster.

The United Irishmen first sought to achieve their aims by radical persuasion and by enlisting mass support. They were neither republicans nor committed to complete independence from Britain. Nor at this stage did they contemplate achieving their ends by violent revolution. It was the intransigence of the Protestant Ascendancy in Ireland, the failure of the British Government to wring sufficient concessions out of the Irish administration, and the increasing willingness of the French to exploit the smouldering resentments in Ireland that combined to drive the society of United Irishmen into the hands of the militant, republican minority. This minority, led by Arthur O'Connor and Lord Edward Fitzgerald, established a new, more secret and oath-bound society willing to establish a republican government by force if necessary. Many Catholics, terrified by sectarian violence which the authorities were unable or unwilling to curb, were prepared to support the militant United Irishmen as a last resort. The militants deliberately sought

46

French military assistance. The French, for their part, were beginning to explore the advantages of intervening in Irish affairs as a means of stretching the military resources of Britain and in revenge for British support for royalist rebels inside France. In 1796 Wolfe Tone and others were sent to France in an effort to convince the French government of the military and diplomatic advantages of intervening in Ireland. These Irish emissaries exaggerated the revolutionary potential in Ireland, claiming that a major rebellion would break out if only the French would first send out a substantial invasion force. Although the militant United Irishmen had gained in determination and purpose they were already becoming over-dependent upon French assistance. An invasion force was increasingly regarded as the essential key to success.

Despite their revolutionary aims and their willingness to contemplate armed rebellion, the new militant society of United Irishmen still suffered from internal divisions, lacked a strong organization and failed to secure mass support. Some attempts were made to build up a military organization and tentative plans were made for an armed rising, but these schemes never developed to the point where the United Irishmen could achieve much on their own. The United Irishmen were in fact never very strong outside Dublin and Belfast. The Catholic Defenders, on the other hand, had much greater numerical support, especially in the rural areas, and had a more effective armed force, but they lacked a clear strategy and a revolutionary ideology. A loose alliance of the two was built up in 1796, but there was never a complete merger. The French for their part were never either able or willing to mount an invasion of the size necessary to ensure success. A significant French force was sent to Ireland in December 1796, but it was dispersed by bad weather and limped back to France without being able to land an effective force. Since there were few regular British troops in Ireland at the time, a golden opportunity was lost. After this disaster the French were reluctant to commit a large military force unless the Irish first embarked on a major rebellion. The Irish were unwilling to risk an armed rising until the French had first put in an appearance. Each side wanted the other to act first.

This situation was ultimately disastrous for all concerned. The leadership of the militant United Irishmen was divided by its inability to launch a rebellion and to secure French backing at the same time. Inactivity split the leadership and shattered the fragile cohesion of the United Irishmen. Indecision and internal bickering meant that no firm lead was given nor clear strategy adopted. Arthur O'Connor and the other leaders had no coherent plan of action, leaving the rank and file to resort to independent but ineffective action. The Irish authorities responded with a determined effort to crush all signs of political disaffection. O'Connor and other leaders were arrested; their main newspaper, the *Northern Star* of Belfast, was closed down; their supporters were disarmed and Ulster was placed under martial law. Some leaders did escape to England or France in order to enlist support in these countries. After several months in prison O'Connor was one leader who eventually made his way to England.

When rebellion did break out in Ireland in 1798 it was largely a popular rising of desperate Catholics determined to protect themselves from the violence of the Orange Order. Although they had conspired to raise a rebellion, the United Irishmen were not in a position to take full advantage of this situation. Internal divisions, the ruthless vigilance of the authorities and the arrest of leaders such as Lord Edward Fitzgerald paralysed the United Irishmen. Never fully geared to the strategy of armed rebellion they were forced to join in a Catholic rebellion in 1798 or risk total annihilation if they stood by and allowed the authorities to crush the rebels. The rebellion started before the United Irishmen had gained control of the situation and their difficulties multiplied when the French failed to arrive. Indecision and confusion reigned among the leadership, while support for their cause was seriously eroded among the Protestant and propertied elements which had once advocated radical reform in Ireland. The rebellion was crushed amid hideous carnage before a small French force put in an appearance.

As a result of this failure, the United Irishmen went into a steep decline from which they never fully recovered. Many of their leaders were arrested. Wolfe Tone committed suicide, but other leaders, including Arthur O'Connor, agreed to confess their guilt in return for an offer from the authorities allowing them to go into exile. While this bargain saved their lives it enabled the Government to prove the existence of a revolutionary conspiracy involving the United Irishmen without having to bring its own spies and informers to court as its star witnesses.

The United Irishmen were unwilling to risk challenging the Protestant Ascendancy again until the French had successfully landed in force. The French were equally determined not to risk another expedition until the United Irishmen had demonstrated their ability to raise a major rebellion. The United Irishmen, still fearful of the Catholics and unable to secure significant support among the Protestants, continued their conspiratorial activities but to little effect. They no longer had a permanent or effective organization within Ireland and most of their leaders were in exile and out of touch with the real situation at home. The Irish authorities continued to infiltrate the small revolutionary groups that survived and arrested the plotters on several occasions. In July 1803 Robert Emmet, realizing that his conspiracy was being discovered, hastily mounted a futile attack on Dublin Castle. He expected the country areas to follow his lead, but there was utter confusion among his followers and the rising was a complete disaster. As in 1798 this resort to armed rebellion intensified the religious divisions within Ireland and led to the further disintegration of the United Irishmen so that they lost any significant base at all in the country. Their leadership was now based entirely on the continent, their effective support in Ireland all but disappeared, and the French never again came to their aid with military support (Elliott, 1982; Wall, 1965).

The United Societies in Britain

The United Irishmen were fully aware that a successful revolution in Ireland depended on events elsewhere. They knew that French military aid was essential, but they also recognized the importance of political subversion in Britain as a means of bringing pressure to bear on the Government there. A successful revolution in Britain would obviously transform the political situation within Ireland itself, but even the threat of armed insurrection would tie down significant forces within Britain and might compel the Government to offer concessions to the Irish radicals. Irish revolutionaries and their emissaries worked therefore not only for French military aid, but for a union of revolutionary forces in Ireland, France and Britain. They travelled through Britain on their way to France and back. Their movements were facilitated by Irish sympathizers in Britain, especially in the north west of England and in the poorer districts of the capital. United Irishmen also stayed in Britain in order to establish firm links with the most militant radical groups in the country and to foment subversive activity. Agents such as William Duckett were establishing contacts as early as 1795 and by late 1796 societies of United Irishmen were being set up in Britain. Missionaries from Ireland visited various parts of England and Scotland in order to establish societies sympathetic to their cause and ready to adopt revolutionary means to achieve radical political reform. In most of these societies Irish immigrants in Britain played an active role. When Arthur O'Connor fled to Britain in 1797 he continued his plans for an armed insurrection from there. He was later joined by the Revd James Coigley, who had come from France

49

with orders to establish contacts with British revolutionary groups.

Thus militant United Irishmen exported revolutionary activity to Britain. Many of their initial contacts and early supporters were Irishmen who had settled in Lancashire, central Scotland and in the poorer areas of London. Nonetheless it is probably going too far to regard revolutionary activity in Britain as largely an Irish import. There had long been a militant minority within the British radical movement and these men were increasingly driven into subversive conspiracies by the Government's repressive policies. As early as December 1792 British newspapers were claiming that only extreme and prompt measures by the Government had nipped in the bud a serious plan for an insurrection in London. There is no convincing proof to show that the new radical societies were definitely implicated in any conspiracy, but there is some evidence to suggest that a few French revolutionaries were in the capital and were endeavouring to foment trouble. Certainly the Government did not fabricate the plot. Ministers were genuinely alarmed and they called up additional troops to London to prevent any insurrection (Emsley, 1978). Over the next years there were scattered rumours of radicals collecting arms and drilling in secret. Robert Watt was actually executed for treason in 1794 for planning an armed attack on Edinburgh castle. It was not until around 1796–7, however, that the more militant British radicals began to contemplate revolution. They were driven to this extreme response by government repression and by the very considerable economic distress caused by high taxation, food shortages and the dislocation of trade. As early as December 1796 Benjamin Binns, a leading member of the LCS, had visited Dublin and established contact with the revolutionary wing of the United Irishmen. Soon, not only were Irish exiles setting up societies of United Irishmen in Britain, but they were also encouraging discontented British radicals to form similar revolutionary groups.

Early in 1797, George Mealmaker of Dundee founded a society of United Scotsmen which adopted the same constitution as the United Irishmen. By May 1797 the society claimed to have 2,871 members in the Dundee and Perth areas, while by September membership was reckoned at 9,653 and still rising. It is very doubtful whether all these members were committed to violent revolution, but some of them were certainly armed and were practising military drill. Their militant behaviour split the radical movement in Scotland. Meanwhile, in Lancashire and adjacent parts of north west England, an organization of United Englishmen had been founded in the spring of 1797. Its members swore a secret oath of loyalty and dedicated themselves to radical parliamentary reform – by force if necessary.

They adopted the structure of the United Irishmen, with groups organized in a pyramidal fashion from local branches through district and county up to provincial levels. As in Scotland their militancy led to a breach with the more moderate radicals in such organizations as the Constitutional Society of Manchester. Also in the North West, as in Scotland, Irish immigrants were actively involved together with other workers who were chiefly employed in the textile industry.

In the summer of 1797 James Coigley, acting as an ambassador of the United Irishmen sent to England by the French Directory, arrived in Manchester to solicit funds and to assess the strength of republicanism in the North West. He appears to have met some thirty-five branch secretaries of the United Englishmen in the area. By the end of the year there were reputed to be some eighty United Englishmen societies, each fifteen to thirty members strong, in Lancashire alone, where William Cheetham (or Chetham) was one of the leading activists. There were also United Englishmen societies in Cheshire, West Yorkshire, Nottinghamshire and Derbyshire, and perhaps in other parts of the Midlands. There can be no doubt about the existence of revolutionary groups, but the network of United Englishmen societies may not have progressed much beyond the preparatory stage before its leaders were arrested. Evidence about their activities comes largely from government agents who were not particularly noted for their reliability at this time, but there is some evidence from arrested United Englishmen themselves. It is unlikely that arming had gone very far, but a willingness to contemplate revolution certainly existed. Most of those implicated in the conspiracy were destitute Irish and English weavers or impoverished spinners, tailors, shoemakers and even labourers. The United Englishmen brought in members from lower down the social scale than the British Jacobin societies had done.

In London the more militant members of the LCS, infuriated by the Government's repressive policies, also began to consider the necessity of a clandestine organization and the expediency of violence. John and Benjamin Binns, John Bone, Thomas Evans and others established links with the United Irishmen in London, including Arthur O'Connor and James Coigley. John Ashley, a former secretary of the LCS who was now in exile, made contact with United Irishmen agents in France. Militants began to establish several revolutionary groups in London, including the Sons of Liberty and the United Britons (who were later known as the United Englishmen). The United Britons, founded early in 1797, had republican aims and hoped for French assistance in the event of all insurrection in England and a simultaneous rebellion in Ireland. Some of its recruits, including Thomas Evans and Alexander Galloway, were prominent members of the LCS. Arms were collected and military drill was practised. Although the United Britons made contact with United Irishmen emissaries, such as James Coigley, and with the United Irishmen societies in the Irish areas of London, they failed to establish a unified command structure or to adopt an agreed policy of action. The Binns brothers did get both the LCS and the United Englishmen to vote addresses in support of Irish grievances and these were taken by Benjamin Binns to Dublin where he had discussions with United Irishmen leaders. In London a central committee, which included the Binns brothers, Colonel Despard and Dr Crossfield, was set up with the task of combining the efforts of the Irish and English revolutionary groups in London. James Coigley again visited Manchester and the North West, early in 1798, in an effort to rally the revolutionary groups there behind those in the capital. There is some evidence of arming and drilling in the North West and of similar activity in Scotland, though efforts there were hampered by the arrest of George Mealmaker and others in Dundee in January 1798.

The authorities were clearly beginning to penetrate the various conspiracies and were shadowing the revolutionary leaders, particularly James Coigley, who were moving about the country seeking to co-ordinate militant action. Although the Government and the leading conspirators themselves exaggerated the extent of popular involvement in the clandestine revolutionary movement, there can be no doubt that plans for an insurrection were being hatched by the beginning of 1798. Whether these plans had any hope of success is another question and may be very seriously doubted. There was certainly no real unity among the various militant groups and no agreed or co-ordinated strategy about when and how an armed uprising was to be staged.

The Government, however, struck hard when it had sufficient evidence that several revolutionary leaders, including James Coigley, Arthur O'Connor and John Binns, were on their way to France to seek French backing for their conspiracy. These men were arrested on 28 February 1798. In London Benjamin Binns, Thomas Evans, Colonel Despard, Dr Crossfield and others were arrested soon afterwards. On 18 April thirteen members of the LCS were arrested while discussing a proposal to form a branch of the United Englishmen, and next day the whole general committee of the LCS was arrested. James Dixon, the Irish leader of the United Englishmen in Manchester, was arrested on 10 April 1798; other conspirators were seized in Lancashire, Scotland and Ireland. Many other revolutionaries went into hiding. The conspiracy, at least in Britain, was temporarily crushed. Because it was unwilling to expose its valuable informants, particularly its spy in Hamburg, the Government could not produce sufficient evidence to convict most of those arrested. Arthur O'Connor was able to call leading Whig MPs as character witnesses, though he seriously embarrassed these men when he subsequently confessed his involvement in the Irish rebellion. Only James Coigley, who was seized while in possession of papers urging a French invasion, was convicted of treason and executed. The Government kept many of those who were acquitted in prison until 1801 when its repressive legislation lapsed and they were released.

The United Englishmen were reported to be reviving in London in the summer of 1798 and the Government was informed by one of its spies that some groups were drilling in the East End, and that attempts were being made to subvert the troops in the capital. There was still no co-ordinated activity with the United Irishmen in London, however, and no British insurrection to divert troops from Ireland where the rebellion of 1798 was being crushed with great savagery. The collapse of the Irish rebellion did lead to hundreds of United Irishmen fleeing the country. Many of them reached London where they were soon involved in further conspiracies. The United Englishmen also revived in London in 1799. The report of the parliamentary secret committee later claimed that there were forty divisions of the United Englishmen in London, of which twenty were particularly active. This was subsequently confirmed by the revolutionaries themselves. Similar revolutionary groups also survived in the North West, in parts of the Midlands and in central Scotland, but they lacked vigour and a coherent strategy. Evidence of their activities is sparse and largely unreliable, but there seems little doubt that some groups continued to exist. All of these groups feared, with considerable justice, that their organizations were still being penetrated by government spies. Certainly arrests continued to be made and the conspirators were reduced to isolated groups holding the occasional secret or nocturnal gathering (Goodwin, 1979, chapter 11; Hone, 1982, chapter 2; Wells, 1983, chapters 3, 4, 6, 7).

The remnants of the revolutionary organizations began to revive during 1801–2, when war weariness, high food prices and economic depression caused widespread discontent. There were reports of United Englishmen and United Irishmen holding meetings in south Lancashire, west Yorkshire and London. Rumours spread of nocturnal gatherings and military drilling on the moors in the North

West where a few hardened conspirators exploited the severe economic distress. The Government quickly destroyed the effectiveness of the revolutionary cells in the area and made a number of arrests. This activity in the North West was sporadic, disorganized and lacking either in a coherent policy or mass support. Nonetheless, combined with renewed activity by the United Irishmen in Britain, it was sufficient to encourage Colonel Despard to plan an armed insurrection in London in 1802. As with so many other conspiracies this plot was soon penetrated by government spies. The authorities discovered the plans to suborn some of the troops in the capital and to seize the Tower, the Bank of England and Woolwich Arsenal. They also learned of delegates being sent to the North West to collect funds and to alert the revolutionary cells there to expect a signal from London which should be followed by a general insurrection. It seems unlikely however that these plans were far advanced or that Colonel Despard was planning to embark on an armed rising as early as November 1802. He and his co-conspirators were almost certainly disposed to wait for another Irish rebellion and for a French invasion before they were prepared to act. In November 1802 the Government decided to take no chances and to nip the conspiracy in the bud. Colonel Despard and several others were arrested. The Government, wary after previous failures, concentrated its attentions upon those against whom it could build up a convincing case without exposing all its informers and agents to cross examination in the witness box (Elliott, 1977). By arresting Despard so early, the Government failed to discover the full extent of the conspiracy, but its success in convicting and executing Despard in 1803 certainly accelerated the decline in English support for a violent revolution. For a few more years some English conspirators appear to have remained convinced of the need for violent revolution, but there is little evidence of co-ordinated activity or a coherent strategy, still less of much popular support during the remaining years of the war with France. Only a successful French invasion could have reactivated the revolutionary conspiracy which smouldered in London and the North West after 1803.

The Political Exploitation of Economic Distress

Economic distress was always a major recruiting agent for the radical cause and a few militant radicals were ready to exploit economic discontent in order to enlist the impoverished masses behind a political reform programme. There are isolated examples of political slogans being shouted by a few of those involved in food riots and industrial strikes, and it seems clear that a few radical activists occasionally tried to inject a political message into popular disturbances which were essentially economic in origin. In general the links between political radicalism and economic disturbances were frail and tenuous. Certainly the radical activists never developed a coherent strategy to capitalize upon the distress of the labouring masses, nor did they manage to exploit the ability of the lower orders to stage their own impressive crowd demonstrations or to organize effective trade unions. Nonetheless, some historians have perceived a significant political dimension in the naval mutinies of 1797, the 'Black Lamp' disturbances of 1801–2 and the widespread Luddite disorders of 1811–13. Other historians have denied that these were anything more than violent protests motivated solely by harsh economic distress.

In many ways one of the most alarmingly subversive developments of the 1790s was the growing disaffection in the Royal Navy, the country's first and most vital line of defence against the French. The initial causes, and no doubt the major precipitants of the mutinies of 1797, were the bitter grievances of the sailors with regard to their poor pay and appalling conditions of service, but the degree of political motivation in these mutinies also needs to be investigated. Inflation in the 1790s had seriously eroded the already low level of wages paid to ordinary seamen in the Royal Navy. The sailors often left impoverished families behind them when they put to sea in defence of their country. The high risks of injury and death at sea greatly increased the chances of their families being left destitute by an ungrateful country which did not properly appreciate the value of the heroic services performed by its sailors. What increased the discontent of most seamen were the appalling conditions of life aboard a man-of-war. The accommodation was cramped and unhealthy, the food became steadily more awful the longer the ship was at sea, and the code of discipline was violent and savage. These undoubted grievances could become grave injustices in some ships where officers physically abused their men and neglected their welfare. Petitions for redress made little headway with the Admiralty and this disregard of long-simmering grievances eventually incited a widespread and alarming mutiny just when the country faced the possibility of invasion. In April 1797 the Channel fleet at Spithead refused to sail until its grievances were redressed and in May the North Sea fleet at the Nore followed this lead. Swift concessions from a thoroughly alarmed Government quickly ended the first mutiny, but at the Nore the seamen were better organized and their greater demands were not so readily met. The sailors elected two delegates

55

from each ship to a central committee chaired by Richard Parker and there was talk of sailing the fleet to France if their demands were not met. Faced with this crisis the Government was more intransigent. It offered some concessions in a deliberate effort to divide the mutineers who were already badly split over what policy to pursue. The mutineers eventually fell to blows, many capitulated in June 1797 and the authorities were able to execute thirty-six of the leaders and to hand out hundreds of lesser sentences.

Even as a simple mutiny the events of 1797 were an alarming indication of the vulnerability of the country, but what really shook the Government was the fear that Jacobin instigators had incited the seamen to revolt. William Pitt, the Prime Minister, appears to have been convinced of this, though the Home Office investigators could find no definite links between the mutineers and political radicals. No mutineer was charged with treasonable political activities. Most modern historians have blamed the mutiny solely on the bad conditions of service in the fleet and they have rejected the idea of any political motivation behind the seamen's actions. In his book, *The Naval Mutinies of 1797*, written in 1913, Conrad Gill did claim that there was a fusion of economic and political causes behind the mutinies. He was impressed by the seamen's organization, language and use of oaths which reflected the structure and practices of the United Irishmen and the LCS. Gill did not investigate these possible connections in any detail, but his claims have been repeated more recently by Edward Thompson. In his view the naval mutinies were the greatest revolutionary portents of the period and he has insisted that a popular revolutionary crisis usually originates in a conjunction between the material grievances of the majority and the aspirations articulated by the politically conscious minority (1968, pp. 183–5). These claims have been reinforced by the more detailed research of Roger Wells (1983, chapter 5). This research highlights the fact that as many as 15,000 out of the total of 114,000 sailors in 1797 were Irishmen, often former members of the United Irishmen or the Defenders, who had been forced into the navy by the Government's endeavours to reduce the number of militant troublemakers in Ireland. There is evidence of cells of United Irishmen being established in the Channel fleet before the mutiny there, and these men sent two delegates to the Nore fleet to incite the Irish seamen serving in its ships. The leaders of the United Irishmen were certainly anxious to exploit the mutinies in order to improve the chances of a successful French invasion of Ireland. They sought to prolong the mutinies and they even urged the more militant Irish mutineers to sail their ships to France.

Not all the leading mutineers were Irishmen, of course, but there is evidence that many of the English mutineers were 'quota men' who had been induced to serve in the fleet by offers of financial bounties by local authorities. These bounties were often accepted by shopkeepers, tradesmen and artisans who were in debt at the time. These men were better educated than most ordinary seamen and they were the type of men to have contact with the radical societies of the period. The organization of the mutineers, with their delegates, ships' committees and central committee, certainly reflects the influence of the radical societies. There was some talk among the mutineers of the need for political changes and some evidence of LCS men visiting the naval dockyards and of radical handbills reaching the fleet. While this evidence is rather sketchy and not entirely reliable it does seem likely that the United Irishmen and the LCS established contact with the fleet and that some mutineers were politically conscious. Nonetheless, the weight of evidence and the actual behaviour of the vast majority of the seamen suggest that the dispute was primarily over pay and conditions and that when these grievances were redressed support for the mutiny quickly collapsed.

Edward Thompson has also argued that the 'Black Lamp' agitation in West Yorkshire in 1801–2 was a mixture of industrial protest and revolutionary conspiracy (1968, pp. 515–28). Although he accepts that genuine economic grievances lay behind much of the disorder among the woollen workers, he believes that the surviving remnants of the United Englishmen in the area exploited the situation for political ends. In his view, the nocturnal gatherings and secret meetings were evidence of clandestine revolutionary preparations. He sees evidence of ulterior political objectives among those who organized the striking workers and he quotes from a revolutionary handbill distributed among the protesters. Thompson rests too much of his argument on the reports of a government agent who was subsequently dismissed for sending in alarmist reports. There is certainly no conclusive evidence that the secret nocturnal meetings were for furthering political conspiracies rather than the economic interests of the workers (Dinwiddy, 1974). Nevertheless, while Thompson may have exaggerated the revolutionary element in working-class agitation in these years, it is probably a mistake to regard economic protests and demands for political reform as two entirely separate phenomena. It should certainly be remembered that the United Englishmen had flourished in the area only a short time before, and that two Sheffield men, William Lee and William Ronkesley, were convicted in 1802 of administering secret oaths and

57

gathering arms. They and others in the area were in contact with the Despard conspirators in London.

After the collapse of the Despard conspiracy and the Black Lamp agitation there is very little evidence of revolutionary activity for a decade, though Edward Thompson has argued that such activity was merely driven underground by repression only to erupt again during the Luddite disturbances of 1811–13. Thompson admits that the Luddites were protesting about genuine economic grievances and that sheer distress produced the mass recruits and the popular sympathy for Luddite protests. On the other hand he insists that 'Luddism was a quasi-insurrectionary movement which continually trembled on the edge of ulterior revolutionary objectives' (1968, p. 604). While it was not a wholly conscious revolutionary movement, it had a tendency to become one. This claim runs counter to the arguments put forward by J. L. and B. Hammond (1979 edition), F. O. Darvall (1934) and Malcolm Thomis (1970). These historians have insisted that there is no clear evidence of Luddite involvement in political conspiracies and no Luddite plan to overthrow the Government by force.

There is considerable agreement about the economic causes of the Luddite protests in Nottinghamshire, south Lancashire and west Yorkshire. In Nottinghamshire and Lancashire the framework knitters and handloom weavers respectively were exposed to various forms of exploitation. They received low wages, paid high rents for their frames or looms, and saw their employers hire semi-skilled labour at lower rates. Only in west Yorkshire did the highly skilled croppers fear that their skills would soon be replaced by the introduction of new machinery, the gig mill and the shearing frame. In all three areas the workers resorted to violent protests only after petitions to Parliament and their own sophisticated workers' organizations had failed to secure the redress of their grievances. Parliament failed to implement or improve the paternalistic legislation which might have protected these workers from exploitation by their employers. Physical attacks on machinery and property were the last resort of men driven to despair by the callousness of their employers and the indifference of the governing elite.

There is general agreement among historians that the Luddite disturbances, the worst of them occurring in 1812, were the result of the failure of more peaceful forms of protest. Darvall and Thomis insist that the Luddites turned to violence as the most effective way of coercing their employers into making concessions by facing them with the prospect of unacceptable financial losses. While these historians admit that arms were seized and were even occasionally ·

used, they claim that these actions were the efforts of militant workers driven to physical action to advance their economic causes, or the work of criminal bands exploiting the disturbed state of the Luddite areas in order to enrich themselves by armed robbery. Reports of secret meetings of disaffected Luddites with political objectives are said to come from tainted sources. Many local magistrates were alarmists who were thoroughly frightened by the impenetrability of the Luddite organization. Many government spies were only employed so long as the disturbance appeared threatening and so they had an interest in exaggerating the seriousness of the disorder. Much of the evidence about arms and drilling was based on rumour and hearsay. While there may have been a handful of political radicals engaged in revolutionary conspiracies in the disturbed areas, it is claimed that they were the ineffective remnants of earlier revolutionary formations and they failed to establish strong links with the rioters or to enlist mass support among the local population. Despite government fears of a deep-laid revolutionary conspiracy, the real threat to order was simply widespread social anarchy and the numerous uncontrolled attacks on employers and their property. The laws were certainly being subverted by highly-organized and well-led bands of Luddites, who enjoyed very considerable local sympathy, but there was no plot to overturn the existing constitution.

Edward Thompson, however, has refused to ignore or discount all the contemporary reports which provide accounts of radical delegates moving through the Luddite areas encouraging the collection of arms and clandestine military drilling in preparation for some future insurrection. In his view a small number of radicals injected a political element into the Luddite disturbances at least in some of the disaffected areas. He accepts that Luddism in Nottinghamshire was almost exclusively an industrial dispute motivated by purely economic grievances, but he insists that in south Lancashire and parts of west Yorkshire the tradition of revolutionary conspiracy and the widespread and bitter hostility to the war in France produced some clandestine political activity and tentative preparations for an armed insurrection. Some Luddites did engage in attacks on the political corruption and the high taxes which resulted from the continuing war with France (Thompson, 1968, pp. 569–659).

John Dinwiddy, who has not always accepted Edward Thompson's evidence of revolutionary activity in this period, has more recently concluded that Thompson was right not to draw a sharp distinction between industrial protests and political action. Often the two forms of behaviour were closely associated and could feed on the same grievances. The failure of industrial action could lead to demands for changes in the political system, while political action might aim at economic improvements. In south Lancashire during 1811 there is clear evidence of determined efforts by the handloom weavers to petition Parliament for a redress of their economic grievances. The weavers' committee in Manchester distributed a printed address in October 1811 which forcefully pointed out the connection between the legislature's refusal to redress their grievances and the need for a radical reform of Parliament. The weavers' petition of March 1812 protested at the continuation of the ruinously expensive war with France and claimed that a reformed Parliament would make peace. The petition had no effect and this appears to have provoked some of the weavers into more militant action. Government spies almost certainly exaggerated developments when they reported that an extensive revolutionary movement was being built up in the area. It seems quite conceivable however that there was some resumption of the kind of clandestine political activity that had existed in this area between 1797 and 1802. Evidence of political committees, secret oaths, nocturnal meetings and the collection of arms and money, especially in the Manchester and Bolton areas, is quite substantial for the early months of 1812. Resolutions and petitions in support of parliamentary reform, and also outbreaks of rioting and attacks on property, spread across the industrial areas of south Lancashire and into the adjacent areas of Cheshire and Yorkshire. There appears to be no clear-cut division between those who participated in the constitutional reform movement, preparing petitions, resolutions and addresses, and those who engaged in violent and clandestine attacks on property. There is evidence, which cannot be entirely discounted, that underground political groups spread their activities into the industrial towns of West Yorkshire, including Halifax, Barnsley, Huddersfield, Sheffield and Leeds. It is unlikely that plans for an armed insurrection were ever very far advanced or that a very extensive revolutionary movement existed, but the available evidence does justify the conclusion that some groups of workers with revolutionary aims were beginning to mobilize in a rudimentary way in the north west of England in 1812 (Dinwiddy, 1979).

There are certainly sufficient grounds for questioning the traditional view that Luddism remained entirely devoid of any tendency to develop into a revolutionary movement with political objectives. Edward Thompson and his disciples may be too prone to exaggerate the scale, the effectiveness, the extent of the support and the sustained activity of the revolutionary movement in the industrial regions of early nineteenth-century England. It is open to doubt

60

whether the revolutionaries ever posed a serious threat or had much hope of becoming a formidable danger to the state. The conspiratorial groups may have been few in number, only loosely connected together, patchily supplied with arms and lacking either a coherent strategy or widespread popular support. Nonetheless, despite these reservations, it is no longer possible to accept that the Luddite disturbances of 1811–12, any more than the naval mutinies of 1797 or the Black Lamp agitation of 1801–2, were solely and simply the product of economic distress and sought only the amelioration of material conditions.

4 Radicalism Relaunched

The radical movement in Britain had expanded in remarkable fashion in the early 1790s, but it had soon been subjected to enormous pressures which had at first stifled its growth and then severely suppressed its activities. Government repression and a wave of loyalist and patriotic sentiment, which gathered force as Britain engaged in a long and bitter armed struggle with revolutionary France, halted the rapid growth of radical societies. The militant radicals were driven underground into clandestine revolutionary conspiracies, but many of their groups were penetrated by government agents and their most serious plots were discovered. The activities of the revolutionaries never resulted in detailed plans, a co-ordinated strategy, mass support or an actual rising outside Ireland. The collapse of the mass radical movement outside Parliament coincided with the decline and disintegration of the reforming element within the Whig party. After the Whig motion for moderate parliamentary reform received only very little support in 1797, the party lost interest in the cause.

Political reform did not again become a subject for serious parliamentary debate, or a cause with widespread public support, for at least a decade, but the desire for greater liberty never entirely disappeared as a topic for discussion. Small groups of reformers continued to operate in many towns, including London, Norwich, Leeds and Newcastle. In 1802 the reformers secured the election of H. C. Combe for London, William Smith for Norwich and Sir Francis Burdett for Middlesex, though the last was eventually unseated on a petition. The subject of reform gradually became a topic of public discussion in newspapers, pamphlets and debating societies. Veteran reformers such as Christopher Wyvill, John Cartwright and John Horne Tooke returned to the fray and were supported by new additions to the cause of the calibre of Francis Burdett, William Cobbett and Henry Hunt. The election of Burdett for Westminster, the largest constituency in the country in 1807, was testimony to the growing strength of radicalism in the large urban areas. When 115 MPs supported Thomas Brand's proposal for a moderate reform of Parliament in May 1810 it was proof that the cause of liberty was again a live issue in politics. Nevertheless, while these are important landmarks in the revival of radicalism, they are also evidence of how far the cause of reform had collapsed since the early 1790s, and how difficult it was going to be to recover all the ground lost in the intervening years. There were clearly favourable circumstances which allowed radicalism to be relaunched, but there were also serious obstacles preventing it from making rapid strides. In coming to terms with these opportunities and these obstacles, radicalism had to readjust its ideology, reorientate its propaganda and rebuild its organization.

Obstacles and Opportunities

The conservative forces which had combined to destroy the effectiveness of the radical movement in the 1790s may have displayed less intense feelings of hatred and fear of reform by the early 1800s, but they had gained a more deep-rooted conviction that radical change was the prelude to disaster. The reports of the parliamentary committees of secrecy of 1799 and 1801, which investigated the revolutionary conspiracies in Britain, did not provoke panic but rather a cold determination to crush any sign of political disaffection. The very serious threat of invasion during 1803–5 did not produce a fearful witch-hunt against the few surviving radicals, but it did arouse a fierce determination to resist the invader and a concurrent tidal wave of patriotic sentiment in support of the established order. The radicals, of course, still faced repression, intimidation and abuse, but it was the ideological argument that they had lost, and both sides were becoming aware of this sea change in the political debate. The ideological dispute between radicals and conservatives had been transformed from a debate about future progress to an argument about present disasters. The tide of events in Europe had destroyed the optimistic hopes of the radicals and had confirmed the pessimistic prognostications of the conservatives.

The radicals had believed that the proclamation of liberty, equality and fraternity would herald an age of reason and justice in which peace and prosperity would flourish. The conservatives had prophesied that revolutionary change would destroy the stability and order of the old regime and would create social anarchy in which no man's life, liberty or property would be secure. Edmund Burke had forecast that the French Revolution would result in a military

63

dictatorship to impose some order on the utter confusion which radical change had brought down upon the people. Events in France, as it moved from the anarchy of the Terror, through the corruption of the Directory, to the military absolutism of Napoleon, confirmed this alarming prophecy. Early sympathizers with the French Revolution, including James Mackintosh, William Wordsworth and Samuel Taylor Coleridge, were gradually convinced that France was not advancing the cause of liberty but exchanging one form of tyranny for another. France had ceased to be a beacon of hope for the peoples of Europe and had instead become an unrestrained aggressor intent on destroying the independence and the civil liberties of one country after another. Napoleon's subjugation of Holland and Switzerland, of large parts of Germany and Italy, and then of Spain, proved to many in Britain that his aim was not to spread liberty abroad but to expand French power throughout Europe. More alarming still was his determination to invade Britain in order to subjugate her to his will or, when this proved impossible, to cripple Britain's economy so that she could never again challenge France's hegemony on the continent. These dangers undermined the appeal of radicalism within Britain and served as an enormous stimulus to British patriotism and nationalism. In many minds the French Revolution was indelibly associated with social anarchy and Napoleon became synonymous with tyranny and military aggression. It became increasingly difficult to sustain the claim that radical reform would produce peace and prosperity, or to maintain that a reactionary British Government was waging an aggressive and unnecessary war on a neighbouring country which simply wished to reform its internal system of government. Britain was now inundated with conservative propaganda, much of it aimed directly at the lower orders, but this literature no longer concentrated so much on challenging the intellectual foundations of the theory of natural rights or attempting to combat the radical claim that the French were friends of liberty. These battles had already been won. The conservatives sought instead to convince the people that plunder and desolation throughout Britain would be the inevitable consequence of a French military victory. To preserve their lives, liberty and property and all that they held dear, the whole British nation must unite in the struggle against the foreign tyrant (Klingsberg and Hustredt, 1944).

Despite the favourable climate for conservatism, the long and expensive war to contain Napoleon's ambitions also created opportunities and circumstances favourable to those who wished to achieve moderate political reforms at home. The burden of the war was enormous and was bitterly resented by large sections of the population. A whole range of new assessed taxes, an inheritance tax and the creation of the hated income tax greatly increased the revenue raised by the Government. By the last years of the war, the Government was levying over £60 million each year in war taxes, but even these sums only met some 58 per cent of expenses. To meet the annual deficits the Government had to raise vast loans which greatly increased the national debt. Gross annual expenditure increased five-fold between 1790 and 1815; the national debt rose from £238 million in 1793 to £902 million in 1816; and the total cost of the war ran to a staggering £1,500 million. To collect and disburse vast sums required a major reorganization and professionalization of the Treasury, the appointment of many more tax collectors and tax inspectors, and a significant expansion of the Ordnance and the naval dockyards. The army and the navy expanded enormously and with the tens of thousands of men serving in the Volunteers and the militia, Britain was supporting an armed force of about 785,000 men. The Government was more involved than ever before in supplying the food, arms, uniforms, ships, horses, equipment and other provisions for these forces. The consequence of all this was that the executive vastly expanded its manpower, its patronage and influence in the financial, commercial and manufacturing affairs of the nation (Harvey, 1978 pp. 334–7; Emsley, 1979b, pp. 106–9). The burdens of the war created widespread resentment. There was public criticism of the high taxes, of the food shortages and the constant inflation which were exacerbated by the continual conflict, and of the dislocation of trade which became particularly severe after 1807–8. All of these direct consequences of war caused suffering among the productive classes in the middling and lower ranks of society. At the same time, the need to mobilize the nation's resources for war also increased the size and patronage of the executive and enriched a minority of war profiteers. War taxation and war borrowing were seen as creating a less equal distribution of wealth in society and as posing a serious threat to political liberty. The financial demands of the war placed a growing tax burden on the majority of the population, but the handling and disbursement of these huge sums benefited financiers, government contractors, government officials and officers in the armed forces. This 'war establishment' was firmly bound by patronage to the ruling oligarchy and this created an interest in the state which exercised very considerable influence over the composition and the decisions of both Parliament and executive. The ruling oligarchy and the war establishment formed an unholy alliance at the expense of the middling and lower orders. This

65

alliance favoured increases in executive power at the expense of both the independence of Parliament and the liberty of the subject.

The war with France had always been opposed on idealistic grounds because of its waste, brutality and destructiveness. To many liberals and Dissenters it was an affront to reason, justice and Christian principles. The growing burden of the war also produced opposition on more pragmatic grounds. Liberal opinion increasingly feared the expansion of the war establishment and the growing power of the executive. At the same time, the manufacturing interest came to resent the disruption of their economic activities by a political establishment which ignored its advice. The result was an alliance of liberal opinion and economic interests united in a campaign for peace. While never a formally constituted body with a declared programme and definite membership, the 'Friends of Peace' organized a sophisticated extra-parliamentary movement that educated the public about the economic and political costs of the war. The most vigorous protests against the war emanated from the manufacturing districts of the Midlands and the North. These were co-ordinated and orchestrated by leading manufacturers, many of whom were Dissenters and were well known for their liberal opinions. They included William Roscoe of Liverpool, Josiah Wedgwood of the Potteries, Ebenezer Rhodes of Sheffield, John Coltman of Leicester and William Strutt of Derby. Their arguments were propagated by influential provincial newspapers such as the *Leeds Mercury*, the *Sheffield Iris* and the *Leicester Chronicle*. In 1807–8 an enormous petitioning campaign was waged against the Orders in Council which threatened to restrict British exports by preventing all neutrals trading with the enemy. These neutrals often bought and carried British goods. Liverpool and Manchester gave a lead to the towns of south Lancashire and these were soon joined by the larger towns of west Yorkshire. Numerous petitions, with over 150,000 signatures, were sent to Parliament. These failed to influence government policy, but, in 1812, at the height of economic distress and Luddite disturbances, another massive protest campaign was launched. Henry Brougham helped to co-ordinate the protests from south Lancashire, west Yorkshire and throughout the Midlands. He bombarded the Government with facts and his allies filled the provincial press with their propaganda. At least 5,000 people attended a protest meeting at Sheffield and many more attended one in Birmingham. Some 50,000 people signed petitions. The Government's decision to revoke the Orders in Council on 23 June 1812 was a tribute to the remarkable co-operation displayed by the most important manufacturing regions of the country (Cookson, 1982).

Protests against the war were not confined to extra-parliamentary campaigns focusing on the economic costs of the conflict with France. There was also considerable criticism, inside and outside Parliament, of the Government's incompetent handling of the war and of the corruption of some of its agents. Military disasters and political scandals highlighted the Government's inadequacies and gave its critics a target on which to focus their frustrations and anger. These incidents also enabled the opposition inside and outside Parliament to lay the blame not only upon individual ministers but upon the political system as a whole. Demands for parliamentary reform were undoubtedly fuelled by public concern about military failures and government corruption.

In August 1808, for example, the British forces in Portugal signed the Convention of Cintra which allowed the evacuation of the defeated French troops, with all their possessions, back to France. On hearing of this, public indignation was bitter and widespread. People in all walks of life were appalled by the betrayal of their hopes and the public prints were full of criticisms of the Convention. Protest meetings were held in various parts of the country and the Government began to lose public credit. A year later the failure of the Walcheren expedition provoked even more public anger and the Government had to face a very damaging committee of inquiry. In an ill-considered attempt to reduce public interest in this inquiry, the ministry sought the exclusion of reporters from the gallery of the House of Commons. When John Gale Jones, a former leading member of the LCS, proposed to discuss this at a London debating society he was arrested for breach of privilege. Sir Francis Burdett protested in the House of Commons against the arrest of Jones and he published his opinions in William Cobbett's *Political Register*. These actions were also condemned as a breach of privilege and the Commons voted, on 6 April 1810, to have Burdett committed to the Tower of London. For three days Burdett refused to submit to arrest and his resistance aroused tremendous public excitement. Large crowds gathered outside Burdett's house, serious rioting broke out and at least two people were killed in clashes with the troops. Political excitement continued after Burdett's imprisonment. Slogans were chalked on walls in London proclaiming 'Burdett for Ever', 'No King' and 'Reform in Parliament and we shall be the masters'. Similar slogans appeared in Birmingham, Newcastle, Carlisle, Exeter and Canterbury. An address to Burdett from Manchester secured 17,940 signatures. The Common Council of London petitioned Parliament in favour of parliamentary reform, the first time it had done so since the 1780s. Similar petitions were organized in Nottingham, Reading, Coventry, Canterbury, Hull, Rochester, Berwick, Worcester and Berkshire. Burdett became a popular martyr for liberty in the manner of John Wilkes and the cause of parliamentary reform was given a tremendous, if temporary, boost (Harvey, 1978, pp. 214–5, 268–70; Dinwiddy, 1980, pp. 20–2).

The demand for parliamentary reform was also stimulated by the growing conviction, inside and outside Parliament, that the Government was turning a blind eye to corruption in high places. Widespread and deep-seated hostility to government patronage and financial corruption flared into major outbursts of public indignation over the Melville scandal in 1805 and the Duke of York affair in 1809. In 1805 a report into the administration of the navy produced evidence of the misappropriation of public funds by the Paymaster of the Navy that had not been prevented by Henry Dundas, Viscount Melville, when he had been Treasurer of the Navy. Although innocent of any direct involvement, Melville was censured by the House of Commons and forced to resign. This did not assuage public indignation. Public meetings were held in a dozen major counties and in several large towns, including London, Westminster, Southampton and Coventry. Petitions were sent to Parliament imploring that the country be saved from rapacity, peculation and fraud. At the Middlesex county meeting, John Cartwright was dissuaded from moving resolutions proposing parliamentary reform, but his passing references to the subject were still met with rapturous applause. Reform sentiment was given a further boost by the parliamentary inquiry into the charge that the Duke of York, the commander-in-chief of the army, had been persuaded by his mistress to sell army commissions to those who bribed her. For months enormous political capital was made out of this public scandal by the small band of parliamentary radicals and their supporters out-of-doors. Members of the middle classes took part in public protest meetings in at least fifteen counties and in no fewer than fifty-six towns. In many places these meetings had the appearance of a revolt against the patrician elite. William Cobbett, who had bitterly attacked the Duke of York in his *Political Register*, helped to carry a violently anti-establishment address in Hampshire. At Liverpool the people were urged to rely upon their own exertions if they were to redress their grievances. On 1 May 1809, some twenty-seven constituencies were represented at a dinner attended by 1,200 people at the Crown and Anchor tavern in London. Among those present were John Cartwright, Francis Place and Robert Waithman. They heard Francis Burdett speak up for parliamentary reform (Harvey, 1978 pp. 155–60, 233–47). Clearly, when sufficiently aroused, the people could express considerable resentment of the patrician elite. Unfortunately, the radicals could never find enough major issues on which to keep public attention sufficiently focused until parliamentary reform became an irresistible demand. Such occasional scandals produced only short-term benefits, but they did indicate a growing disenchantment among the middling orders with the political elite.

Ideology and Propaganda

The reform movement which revived in the early years of the nineteenth century was more moderate in its ideology and aimed its propaganda primarily, though not exclusively, at the middle classes. Of course, government repression and the hostile climate to radical ideas made it difficult to continue public discussion of natural rights theories, but there does appear to have been much less public interest in such extreme notions at this time. Even among the reformers, little interest was now shown in the political ideas of such writers as Paine, Godwin and Spence who had attracted so much attention in the 1790s. Paine's influence had largely collapsed, though it revived more after 1815. Godwin's influence was so short-lived that Shelley was surprised to find him still alive in 1812. Spence still peddled his Land Plan, but his works now had a tiny circulation and he was only able to influence a small group of disciples who met with him in a London tavern.

To a surprising extent the lead in the reviving debate on parliamentary reform was taken by veteran reformers whose careers went back to the age of Wilkes and the American Revolution. John Cartwright, Christopher Wyvill, Capel Lofft, John Horne Tooke, and other old campaigners, now came back to the fore. Moreover, these reformers often returned to the earlier ideas of the radical movement which they believed had gained new relevance. John Cartwright and John Horne Tooke both revived notions of England's ancient constitution and claimed that radical reform would restore the electoral system to its earlier purity and would lead to the recovery of the people's traditional rights. They appealed once more to the historic rights of Englishmen rather than to the inalienable natural rights of all men. This appeal to the ancient constitution, which had a long and respected history, influenced such radical MPs as Francis Burdett and Thomas Brand. When they introduced their motions for parliamentary reform, in 1809 and in 1810 and 1812 respectively, they insisted that they did not wish to alter or remodel the constitution, but to remove recent innovations and to restore ancient electoral practices.

Even more significant than these renewed appeals to the ancient constitution was the revival of traditional country attitudes towards the growth of executive tyranny and the expansion of government patronage. Arguments expressing such fears had been heard over the last two centuries and they had been at the root of long-standing demands for economical reform. The effects of the great war against France led to a renewed concern about the Government's ability to exploit its vast patronage in order to undermine the independence of Parliament and the liberties of the subject. Growing alarm about a government conspiracy against liberty in turn fuelled renewed demands for the old solution of economical reform and parliamentary reform. It was again argued, as it had frequently been argued in the past, that measures must be taken to reduce taxation, the national debt, the size of the civil and military establishments, and the number of government placemen and pensioners who sat in Parliament. Only by legislation to curtail government patronage, and reforms to increase popular influence over the House of Commons, could the old harmonious balance of the constitution be restored. Christopher Wyvill, who had founded the Yorkshire Association in 1779 in order to pursue such policies, was convinced that his remedies were more necessary than ever because of the immediate and drastic consequences of the long conflict with France. In 1804 he was supporting Burdett in his Middlesex election campaign, by December 1805 he was seeking the support of Charles James Fox for his ideas, and by late 1806 he had produced a detailed plan of reform. John Cartwright, although wanting a more radical solution than Wyvill, agreed with his diagnosis of the alarming threat to liberty posed by executive corruption and government patronage. He gave vent to these fears in his *Reasons for Reformation* in 1809.

The most active propagandist for a reduction in patronage and corruption was not a veteran reformer, however, but a former supporter of the administration and its conservative policies. This was William Cobbett who was to become the most prolific and influential radical propagandist of the early nineteenth century. Cobbett had written several pamphlets in defence of government policies and, since 1802, his weekly *Political Register* had praised the existing constitution and justified the need for war with France. In 1804, however, he was convicted for libel for criticizing the government's policy in Ireland and the lack of adequate preparations to meet a French invasion. This personal taste of government repression started his conversion to radicalism. By 1806 he had become a convinced opponent of political corruption. His *Political Register* launched into a bitter and prolonged denunciation of the vast patronage system, with its extensive and ever-growing distribution of jobs, honours, contracts, promotions, pensions and bribes. He published numerous weekly letters to his readers in which he condemned ministers for presiding over a system that corrupted politicians, financiers, contractors, civil servants, officers in the armed services and even clergymen. Horrified by the burden of taxation and the size of the national debt, Cobbett maintained that this financial system allowed a few men in positions of power to enrich themselves whilst beggaring the nation. He denounced stockjobbers, brokers, contractors, bankers and all those who enriched themselves by their financial contacts with the Government. In Cobbett's opinion these upstarts climbed into positions of power from humble origins, not because of any personal merits, but because they profited from the war. It was in their interest to promote high taxes, government extravagance, paper credit, financial speculation, a swollen bureaucracy and widespread political corruption. If not restrained they would destroy the constitution and erode the foundations of the moral and social order of the country (Spater, 1982, chapters 9, 11–15).

It was Cobbett's ability to explain the dangers of corruption in vivid and dramatic language that accounts for his growing influence with the farmers, shopkeepers and tradesmen who read his *Political Register*. The *Edinburgh Review*, a journal which appealed to the liberal element within Parliament and the more intellectual middle classes in the country, condemned Cobbett's coarse language and rejected his political extremism, but it shared his alarm over the growth of executive power and government patronage. In July 1809 Francis Jeffrey used the pages of the *Edinburgh Review* to criticize the burden of taxation, to express concern about the expanding sources of patronage available to the Government, and to attack the way a small minority monopolized political power in the state. In later issues the *Edinburgh Review* campaigned for economical reforms to reduce the Government's ability to influence Parliament and favoured a modest extension of the franchise and a limited redistribution of parliamentary seats. From January 1808, Leigh Hunt propagated similar views in *The Examiner*, whose sales rose to around 12,000 copies by 1812. Hunt praised the principles of the British constitution and rejected radical parliamentary reform, but he shared Cobbett's alarm over government corruption. *The Examiner* was critical of the war with France, which Hunt regarded as the principal engine increasing the size, resources and expenses of

71

the Government. It joined in the attacks on the Duke of York in 1809 and regularly denounced government extravagance as a source of political corruption. Leigh Hunt advocated economical reform and favoured extending the franchise to tax-paying householders.

Fear of executive power and government corruption was the greatest influence operating on the reformers of the early nineteenth century, but there are indications that a new intellectual influence was emerging in radical circles. This was the utilitarian justification for parliamentary reform being developed by Jeremy Bentham, whose influential *Plan of Parliamentary Reform* was in private circulation from 1809, though not published until 1817. Bentham's ideas were becoming known to a growing circle of admirers including Leigh Hunt, Francis Place, John Horne Tooke and Francis Burdett, long before they became public property. By 1813 Bentham was closely connected with the metropolitan radicals and his ideas began to shape their justification for parliamentary reform. Bentham completely rejected the doctrine of natural rights, but he still reached the conclusion that parliamentary reform was essential as the most effective means of preventing misgovernment and ensuring the greatest happiness of the greatest number. His utilitarian philosophy led him to assert that every man prefers his own interest above that of others and that each man is the best judge of his own interests. Since every individual is the best judge of his own interests, then all individuals together must be regarded as the best judges of the public interest. Unfortunately, by the same argument, all governments are more interested in serving the interests of the governors rather than those of the governed. To prevent this abuse of power the governors needed to be continually watched and every device used to ensure that they promoted the welfare of the governed. The most effective way of making the governors serve the proper end of government, which was to promote the greatest happiness of the greatest number, was to allow every man an equal right to judge and control the actions of those in power. Only if Parliament was elected by all the people would representatives be keen to promote the public good, since this would be the best means of securing re-election. Thus, his utilitarian principles led Bentham to the conclusion that representative democracy was the most effective system both for restricting the self-interest of the governors and for promoting the welfare of the greatest number of the governed. Parliamentary reform was therefore justified on practical, expedient and utilitarian grounds.

Aims and Methods

There were many reasons for criticizing the governments of the early nineteenth century, and there was growing concern among the middling ranks of society about the dangers of political corruption. Nonetheless, the widespread fear of revolution and the entrenched conservatism of the propertied elite made it difficult to agree on how best to reform the constitution and how to rally support for such measures. The reformers were divided in their aims between those who would have been satisfied to curtail government patronage, those who wanted a moderate extension of the franchise and a limited redistribution of seats, and those who still supported the full radical six-point programme of parliamentary reform. There was even greater fragmentation among the reformers about how to recruit public support for their views, between those who looked to the means which would enlist only the more prosperous and educated middle classes and those who sought to devise methods of arousing the whole nation.

The opposition Whigs in Parliament, despite their own vociferous complaints about executive tyranny and the growth of corruption, were very timid and cautious about supporting the policy of parliamentary reform. They condemned the radicals outside Parliament as mischievous and misguided men who sought to overawe the legislature by exciting public indignation and clamour. For much of the time they adopted a policy of masterly inactivity and they were not disturbed when demands for reform declined after 1812. The assassination of Spencer Perceval, the violence of the Luddite disturbances, and the dramatic military developments on the continent all helped to shift parliamentary attention away from political reform. Nonetheless, the parliamentary Whigs had to come to terms with the fact that they were now faced with the task of having to co-operate with a body of radical or progressive MPs if they were ever to secure a majority in Parliament. The radical group in Parliament only numbered two dozen or so MPs, the most prominent being Francis Burdett, Thomas Brand, Samuel Whitbread, Samuel Romilly, Henry Brougham, Lord Cochrane, Thomas Creevey, Peter Moore, W. A. Madocks and G. L. Wardle. These men supported economical reform and a moderate measure of parliamentary reform. In 1809 Burdett had advocated more frequent elections, equal-sized constituencies and an extension of the franchise to all male householders who paid direct taxes to the state, the church and the poor. This was regarded as too radical and Burdett's motion was supported by a mere twelve votes. Thomas Brand

73

introduced a more moderate proposal a year later; his scheme would have extended the franchise in a similar way but it would only have redistributed seats from some of the rotten boroughs to the large towns. This motion secured the backing of 115 MPs, the highest support for reform since 1785 and the highest for many years to come.

Outside Parliament, Burdett was still regarded as an extremist by such publications as the *Edinburgh Review* and Leigh Hunt's *Examiner*, and by such reformers as Christopher Wyvill, but there were more reformers of his persuasion. Francis Place and many of the Westminster radicals shared Burdett's desire to enfranchise the propertied middle classes, especially the small merchants, shop-keepers and master craftsmen. Despite his earlier membership of the LCS, Place had turned his back on popular democracy. John Cartwright, however, still advocated universal manhood suffrage, though he occasionally compromised his principles to secure unity in the radical movement. William Cobbett and the young Henry Hunt were determined to pursue only a very radical reform programme. These leading spokesmen for the radical cause shared one thing in common. They were all supreme egotists whose competing ambitions and clashing personalities made it extremely difficult to agree on a radical programme or on the best means of achieving it.

The extra-parliamentary reform movement depended heavily on the energy and the propaganda of a handful of radicals – men such as Burdett, Cartwright, Cobbett and Place. Unfortunately, these spokesmen for parliamentary reform failed to devise a firm organizational base from which to recruit mass support. Their greatest success was in propagating their views in individual pamphlets, in journals such as the *Political Register* and the *Statesman*, and in a growing number of sympathetic provincial newspapers including the *Leeds Mercury*, the *Leicester Chronicle*, the *Sheffield Iris*, the *York Herald*, the *Tyne Mercury* and the *Nottingham Review*. In terms of permanent political organizations however the radicals of this period lagged behind the achievements of earlier years. The refounding of debating societies and a few short-lived political clubs were a poor substitute for the radical societies of the 1790s. There were, however, a few signs of improved organization. These achieved only limited success at first, but they augured well for the future.

In 1807 a group of about twenty activists, including Francis Place, John Richter, Paul Lemaitre, William Adams, George Pullar and Samuel Brooks, formed the Westminster Committee to secure the election of Burdett as an independent candidate in opposition to candidates from the established parliamentary parties. Burdett agreed to stand on condition that he contributed no money, did not canvass for support and did not appear on the hustings. As a wealthy patrician he wished to remain aloof from the humble shopkeepers and tradesmen, some of them former members of the LCS, who hoped to organize his election. Westminster was the largest parliamentary borough in the country, with about 17,000 ratepayers being eligible to vote. This was too large an electorate to be bribed or to be under secure influence, consequently the constituency had a history of 'independent' candidates. The members of the Westminster Committee, though they had no formal organization, were determined to wage a struggle of the smaller men of property against the elite of wealth, rank and influence. Resentful of the social and economic barriers between the aristocratic elite of Westminster and the shopkeepers and tradesmen who supplied their needs, they urged the Westminster voters to demonstrate their independence of their supposed superiors. The Westminster Committee hoped to advise and even direct Burdett as an MP, though he was never a man to serve mere tradesmen electors. Though the Committee had limited funds to fight the election they made up for this with enormous energy and impressive efficiency in canvassing a high proportion of the electors. With the aid of Cobbett's *Political Register* they propagated their radical views throughout the constituency. The result was a remarkable electoral success, with Burdett heading the poll, and Lord Cochrane, another reformer, coming second. This was an important breakthrough and a lesson for the future, but it was not followed up by similar achievements in the other large urban constituencies. Burdett and Cochrane also lacked the energy and the ambition to lead an active group of radicals in the House of Commons (Main, 1966).

Some of the leading metropolitan radicals also worked hard to set up more permanent political associations in the capital and elsewhere. In 1811, Thomas Northmore suggested the establishment of a new political society, to be named the Hampden Club, to work exclusively for parliamentary reform. Northmore stressed the importance of recruiting men of property and he suggested that members should possess the same substantial property qualifications as MPs. He was encouraged by Burdett, but opposed by his friend John Cartwright, who criticized the exclusive nature of the club's proposed membership and suspected such men of lacking a genuine commitment to radical reform. Cartwright himself favoured a radical programme of parliamentary reform and wanted to secure massive popular support for such a platform. He eventually became a member of the Hampden Club in the spring of 1812, but he then resigned in June 1812 to promote a rival political association. It was not until May 1813 that he rejoined the Hampden Club in an effort to combine forces with the supporters of more limited parliamentary reform.

In the intervening period, Cartwright had laboured to establish an alternative radical society. In June 1812 he tried to resuscitate the Committee of the Friends of Parliamentary Reform which he had first founded in 1808. It was now to be known as the Union for Parliamentary Reform according to the Constitution, or more simply, as the Union Society. This society favoured a more radical political programme than the Hampden Club, but it still did not commit itself to universal manhood suffrage nor did it seek to be a mass organization. It demanded the vote for all males paying direct taxes and favoured annual Parliaments. Its annual subscriptions of three guineas kept out all the lower orders. Although William Cobbett, George Wardle MP and the young Henry Hunt agreed to join, the Union Society languished because of its failure to enlist one hundred sponsors. It was this failure and a conviction that the small group of leading radicals must combine forces that persuaded Cartwright to rejoin the Hampden Club. By 1814 Cartwright had won over the Hampden Club to his more radical programme, but only at the cost of a severe reduction in membership. In December 1814 only three members attended the Hampden Club's dinner, and in March 1815 Cartwright dined there alone.

Evidently London was not yet ready for the revival of radical societies, but Cartwright was to show the way forward with his success in the provinces. Because of his failure in the capital, Cartwright turned to the working masses in the provinces. Unlike most of the other radical activists he was ready to trust the ordinary people. He was certainly the only metropolitan radical to stump the country at this time. Relying heavily on his own finances and efforts, though with some support from a few friends and his secretary, Thomas Cleary, Cartwright first toured the Manchester area in the summer of 1812. He visited several manufacturing centres, seeking out local leaders who could be instructed in how to set up a political society and district committees, how to exploit the press for reform propaganda and how to organize groups of volunteer workers who would secure mass support for petitions in favour of parliamentary reform. A branch of the Union Society was founded in Halifax in October 1812 and within two months some 17,000 people there had signed a petition for parliamentary reform. Cartwright certainly encouraged radical activity in the area, but to some extent he was already preaching to the converted. The area had a tradition of political radicalism, it was wracked with Luddite disturbances, and the devastating impact on the cotton industry of the Orders in Council was already stimulating renewed interest in parliamentary reform. In May 1812 a petition from Preston had protested at the Government's extravagant expenditure of public money, and a few days later a meeting in Manchester condemned the ruinously expensive war with France and demanded a radical reform of Parliament.

After his initial success Cartwright drafted the text of a petition to serve as a model for those with no experience of petitioning Parliament. He had this printed and he distributed it in great numbers on his second missionary tour in 1813. On this trip he covered 900 miles in twenty-nine days and he visited no fewer than thirty-four urban communities, including Leicester, Huddersfield, Sheffield, Manchester, Leeds, Preston, Bolton, Liverpool, Stockport, Newcastle, Birmingham, Gloucester, Bristol and Reading. It was a remarkable achievement. Although he did not have time to supervise the actual organization of the petitions, he was able to establish important contacts with many provincial reformers and to deposit batches of his printed petitions with sympathetic gentlemen, ministers of religion, merchants, professional men and respectable tradesmen. Cartwright claimed to have obtained 130,000 signatures from his 1813 tour in favour of petitions requesting a taxpaying householder franchise and annual Parliaments. Thirty thousand people signed the Manchester petition and other petitions came in from most of the places which he visited (Miller, 1968 and 1974).

Cartwright's efforts were to bear their greatest fruit after 1815 when he spread Hampden clubs and Union societies to many parts of the industrial Midlands and North of England, and when he secured popular support on an impressive scale for the cause of radical parliamentary reform. His early missionary tours were already an indication of the growing public dissatisfaction with the unreformed electoral system and its political and economic consequences. Cartwright helped to demonstrate the potential for severe economic distress to be converted into mass political awareness. After 1815, the ending of the war and the French threat to Britain removed a powerful obstacle in the way of radical action. At the same time a severe economic depression encouraged renewed concentration on internal affairs and provided an issue which could focus mass discontent on the need for parliamentary reform. Radicalism flourished after 1815, but it built on the achievements of the reformers who had kept the cause of reform alive in the less auspicious years at the beginning of the nineteenth century.

References and Further Reading

Baxter, J. L. and Donnelly, F. K. 1974: The Revolutionary 'Underground' in the West Riding: Myth or Reality? *Past and Present*, 64, 124–32.

Baylen, J. O. and Gossman, N. J. (eds) 1979: *Biographical Dictionary of British Radicals: Volume 1, 1770–1830*. Brighton: Harvester Press.

Bennett, Betty T. 1976: *British War Poetry in the Age of Romanticism 1793–1815*. New York: Garland Publications.

Bewley, Christina 1981: *Muir of Huntershill*. Oxford: Oxford University Press.

Birley, Robert 1924: *The English Jacobins from 1789 to 1802*. Oxford: Oxford University Press.

Black, E. C. 1963: *The Association: British Extraparliamentary Political Organization, 1769–1793*. Cambridge, Mass: Harvard University Press.

Bohstedt, John 1983: *Riots and Community Politics in England and Wales, 1790–1810*. Cambridge, Mass: Harvard University Press.

Booth, Alan 1977: Food Riots in the North-West of England 1790–1801. *Past and Present*, 77, 84–107.

Booth, Alan 1983: Popular loyalism and public violence in the north-west of England, 1790–1800. *Social History*, 8, 295–313.

Brown, P. A. 1965: *The French Revolution in English History*. London: Frank Cass. Reprint of 1918 edn.

Butler, Marilyn 1984: *Burke, Paine, Godwin, and the Revolution Controversy*. Cambridge: Cambridge University Press.

Calhoun, Craig 1982: *The Question of Class Struggle: Social Foundations of Popular Radicalism during the Industrial Revolution*. Oxford: Blackwell.

Cannon. John 1973: *Parliamentary Reform 1640–1832*. Cambridge: Cambridge University Press.

Christie, I. R. 1984: *Stress and Stability in Late Eighteenth-Century Britain*. Oxford: Clarendon Press.

Cobban, Alfred (ed.) 1960: *The Debate on the French Revolution 1789–1800*. London: A. & C. Black. 2nd edn.

Collins, H. 1954: The London Corresponding Society. In John Saville (ed.), *Democracy and the Labour Movement*. London: Lawrence and Wishart, 103–34.

Cone, Carl B. 1968: *The English Jacobins*. New York: Scribners.

Cookson, J. E. 1982: *The Friends of Peace: anti-war liberalism in England, 1793–1815*. Cambridge: Cambridge University Press.

Darvall, F. O. 1934: *Popular Disturbances and Public Order in Regency England*. London: Oxford University Press.

Dickinson, H. T. 1977: *Liberty and Property: Political Ideology in Eighteenth Century Britain*. London: Weidenfeld and Nicolson. Methuen paperback, 1979.

Dickinson, H. T. (ed.) 1982: *The Political Works of Thomas Spence*. Newcastle upon Tyne: Avero Publications.

Dinwiddy, J. R. 1971: *Christopher Wyvill and Reform 1790–1820*. York: Borthwick Institute of Historical Research. Borthwick Papers No. 39.

Dinwiddy, J. R. 1973: The 'Patriotic Linen Draper': Robert Waithman and the revival of radicalism in the City of London, 1795–181. *Bulletin of the Institute of Historical Research*, 46, 72–94.

Dinwiddy, J. R. 1974: The 'Black Lamp' in Yorkshire 1801–1802. *Past and Present,* 64, 113–23.

Dinwiddy, J. R. 1975: Bentham's Transition to Political Radicalism, 1809–10. *Journal of the History of Ideas*, 36, 683–700.

Dinwiddy, J. R. 1979: Luddism and politics in the northern counties. *Social History*, 4, 3–63.

Dinwiddy, J. R. 1980: Sir Francis Burdett and Burdettite Radicalism. *History*, 65, 17–31.

Donnelly, F. K. and Baxter, J. L. 1975: Sheffield and the English Revolutionary Tradition 1791–1820. *International Review of Social History*, 20, 398–423.

Dozier, Robert R. 1983: *For King, Constitution and Country: The English Loyalists and the French Revolution*. Lexington: University Press of Kentucky.

Elliott, Marianne 1977: The 'Despard Conspiracy' Reconsidered. *Past and Present*, 75, 46–61.

Elliott, Marianne 1982: *Partners in Revolution: The United Irishmen and France*. London: Yale University Press.

Emsley, Clive 1978: The London 'Insurrection' of December 1792: fact, fiction or fantasy? *Journal of British Studies*, 17, 66–86.

Emsley, Clive 1979a: The home office and it sources of information and investigation 1791–1801. *English Historical Review*, 94, 532–61.

Emsley, Clive, 1979b: *British Society and the French Wars 1793–1815*. London: Macmillan.

Emsley, Clive 1981: An Aspect of Pitt's 'Terror': prosecutions for sedition during the 1790s. *Social History*, 6, 155–84.

Fennessy, R. R. 1963: *Burke, Paine and the Rights of Man*. The Hague: Martinus Nijhoff.

Freeman, Michael 1980: *Edmund Burke and the Critique of Political Radicalism*. Oxford: Blackwell.

George, M. Dorothy 1927–9: The Combination Laws Reconsidered. *Economic History*, a supplement to *The Economic Journal*, 1, 214–28.

George, M. Dorothy 1959: *English Political Caricature: A Study of Opinion and Propaganda 1793–1832*. Oxford: Oxford University Press.

Gill, C. 1913: *The Naval Mutinies of 1797*. Manchester: Manchester University Press.

Ginter, D.E. 1966: The Loyalist Association Movement of 1792–93 and British Public Opinion. *Historical Journal*, 9, 179–90.

Goodwin, Albert 1979: *The Friends of Liberty: The English Democratic Movement in the Age of the French Revolution*. London: Hutchinson.

Halévy, Elie 1972: *The Growth of Philosophic Radicalism*. London: Faber and Faber. Reprint of 1934 edn.

Hammond, J. L. and B. 1979: *The Skilled Labourer*. London: Longman. Reprint of 1920 ed.

Hampsher-Monk, Iain 1979: Civic Humanism and Parliamentary Reform: The Case of the Society of the Friends of the People. *Journal of British Studies*, 18, 70–89.

Handforth, P. 1956: Manchester radical politics, 1789–94. *Transactions of the Lancashire and Cheshire Antiquarian Society*, 66, 87–106.

Harvey, A. D. 1978: *Britain in the Early Nineteenth Century*. London: Batsford.

Hawke, David Freeman 1974: *Paine*. New York: Harper and Row.

Hole, Robert 1983: British Counter-revolutionary Popular Propaganda in the 1790s. In Colin Jones (ed.), *Britain and Revolutionary France: Conflict, Subversion and Propaganda*, Exeter: University of Exeter, 53–69.

Hone, J. Ann 1982: *For the Cause of Truth: Radicalism in London 1796–1821*. Oxford: Oxford University Press.

Jewson, C. B. 1975: *The Jacobin City: A Portrait of Norwich in its Reaction to the French Revolution 1788–1802*. London: Blackie.

Jones, Colin 1983: *Britain and Revolutionary France: conflict, subversion and propaganda*. Exeter: University of Exeter.

Klingsberg, F. J. and Hustredt, S. B. (eds) 1944: *The Warning Drum: The British Home Front Faces Napoleon*. Los Angeles: Williams Andrews Clark Memorial Library.

Knight, Frida 1957: *The Strange Case of Thomas Walker*. London: Lawrence and Wishart.

Laprade, W. T. 1909: *England and the French Revolution, 1789–1797*. Baltimore: Johns Hopkins University Press.

Locke, Don 1980: *A Fantasy of Reason: the life and thought of William Godwin*. London: Routledge & Kegan Paul.

Lottes, Günther 1979: *Politische Aufklärung und plebejisches Publikum: zur Theorie und Praxis des englischen Radikalismus im späten 18 Jahrhundert*. Munich: R. Oldenbourg Verlag.

McCord, N. and Brewster, D. E. 1968: Some Labour Troubles of the 1790s in North East England. *International Review of Social History*, 13, 366–83.

McDowell, R. B. 1940: The Personnel of the Dublin Society of United Irishmen, 1791–4. *Irish Historical Studies*, 1, 12–53.

McKenzie, L. A. 1981: The French Revolution and English Parliamentary Reform: James Mackintosh and the *Vindiciae Gallicae*. *Eighteenth-Century Studies*, 14, 264–82.

Main, J. M. 1966: Radical Westminster, 1807–1820. *Historical Studies (Australia and New Zealand)*, 12, 186–204.

Marshall, Peter H. 1984: *William Godwin*. London: Yale University Press.

Meikle, H. W. 1969: *Scotland and the French Revolution*. London: Frank Cass. Reprint of 1912 edn.

Miller, N. C. 1968: John Cartwright and radical parliamentary reform 1808–1819. *English Historical Review*, 83, 705–28.

Miller, N. C. 1974: Major John Cartwright and the Founding of the Hampden Club. *Historical Journal*, 17, 615–9.

Mitchell, Austin 1961: The Association Movement of 1792–3. *Historical Journal*, 4, 56–77.

Money, John 1977: *Experience and Identity: Birmingham and the West Midlands 1760–1800*. Manchester: Manchester University Press.

O'Gorman, F. 1967: *The Whig Party and the French Revolution*. London: Macmillan.

Osborne, John W. 1972: *John Cartwright*. Cambridge: Cambridge University Press.

Pakenham, T. 1968: *The Year of Liberty: The Great Irish Rebellion of 1798*. London: Hodder & Stoughton.

Patterson, M. W. 1931: *Sir Francis Burdett and His Times 1770–1844*. 2 vols. London: Macmillan.

Prochaska, F. K. 1973: English State Trials in the 1790s: A Case Study. *Journal of British Studies*, 13, 63–82.

Rapp, Dean 1982: The Left-Wing Whigs: Whitbread, the Mountain and Reform, 1809–1815. *Journal of British Studies*, 21, 35–66.

Roberts, Michael 1939: *The Whig Party 1807–1812*. London: Macmillan.

Rose, R. B. 1960: The Priestley Riots of 1791. *Past and Present*, 18, 68–88.

Royle, E. and Walvin, J. 1982: *English Radicals and Reformers 1760–1848*. Brighton: Harvester Press.

Seaman, A. W. L. 1957: Radical Politics at Sheffield, 1791–1797. *Transactions of the Hunter Archaeological Society*, 7, 215–28.

Smith, A. W. 1955: Irish Rebels and English Radicals 1798–1820. *Past and Present*, 7, 78–85.

Spater, George 1982: *William Cobbett: The Poor Man's Friend*. 2 vols. Cambridge: Cambridge University Press.

Stern, Walter M. 1964: The Bread Crisis in Britain, 1795–1796. *Economica*, 31, 168–87.

Stevenson, J. 1971: The London 'Crimp' Riots of 1794. *International Review of Social History*, 16, 40–58.

Stevenson, J. 1974: Food Riots in England 1792–1818. In J. Stevenson and R. Quinault (eds), *Popular Protest and Public Order*, London: Allen & Unwin, 33–74.

Stout, G. D. 1949: *The Political History of Leigh Hunt's Examiner*. Saint Louis: Washington University Press.

Thale, Mary (ed.) 1983: *Selections from the Papers of the London Corresponding Society 1792–1799*. Cambridge: Cambridge University Press.

Thomis, M. I. 1970: *The Luddites: Machine-Breaking in Regency England*. Newton Abbot: David & Charles.

Thomis, M. I. and Holt, P. 1977: *Threats of Revolution in Britain 1789–1848*. London: Macmillan.

Thompson, E. P. 1968: *The Making of the English Working Class*. Harmondsworth: Penguin Books.

Tomalin, Claire 1974: *The Life and Death of Mary Wollstonecraft*. London: Weidenfeld & Nicolson.

Veitch, G. S. 1965: *The Genesis of Parliamentary Reform*. London: Constable. Reprint of 1913 edn.

Wall, Maureen 1965: The United Irish Movement. In J. M. McCracken (ed.), *Historical Studies*, London: Bowes & Bowes, 5, 123–40.

Wallas, Graham 1951: *The Life of Francis Place 1771–1854*. 4th edn, London: Allen & Unwin.

Wells, Roger 1977a: *Dearth and Distress in Yorkshire 1793–1802*. York: Borthwick Institute of Historical Research. Borthwick Papers, No. 52.

Wells, Roger 1977b: The revolt of the south-west: a study in English popular protest. *Social History*, 6, 713–44.

Wells, Roger 1983: *Insurrection: The British Experience 1795–1803*. Gloucester: Alan Sutton.

Western, J. R. 1956: The Volunteer Movement as an Anti-Revolutionary Force, 1793–1801. *English Historical Review*, 71, 603–14.

Williams, Gwyn A. 1968: *Artisans and Sans-Culottes: Popular Movements in France and Britain during the French Revolution*. London: Edward Arnold.

Index

Church and King clubs, 32–4
Cintra, Convention of, 67
Cleary, Thomas, 76
clubs, *see* societies
Cobbett, William, 39, 62, 67, 68, 70, 71, 74, 75, 76
Cochrane, Thomas, Lord, 73, 75
Coigley, James, 39, 49, 51, 52, 53
Coleridge, Samuel Taylor, 64
Collins, Henry, 10
Coltman, John, 66
Combe, H. C., 62
committees of secrecy, 40, 43, 63
Commons, House of, 5, 7, 15, 20, 27, 40, 67, 68, 70, 75
Constitution, 4, 5, 14, 15, 26, 27, 34, 42, 71
Constitutional societies, 4, 12–13, 51
Convention, National, 21–2, 38
Cookson, J. E., 66
Cooper, Thomas, 12
Copenhagen House, 23, 24
Coventry, 68
Crossfield, Dr Robert, 11, 52
Crown and Anchor tavern, 33, 68
Crown Office, 39
Cruickshank, Isaac, 30
Cumberland, 33

Darvall, F. O., 58
Defenders, Catholic, 47, 56
Derby, 11, 12, 19, 66
Derby Mercury, 19
Derbyshire, 51
Despard, Colonel Edward, 39, 40, 52, 54, 58
Dickinson, H. T., 7, 17, 18, 29
Dinwiddy, John, 44, 57, 59, 60, 68
Directory, French, 51, 64
Dissenters, 6, 12, 13, 32, 44, 66
Dixon, James, 52
Dozier, Robert, 34, 36
Drennan, Dr William, 45
Dublin, 21, 45, 47, 49, 50, 52
Duckett, William,
Dundas, Henry, later Viscount Melville, 37, 68

Dundee, 12, 50, 52

Eaton, Daniel Isaac, 11, 20, 30, 39, 40
economical reform, 4, 5, 8, 70, 71, 73
Edinburgh, 1, 12, 21, 22, 38, 39, 50
Edinburgh Review, 71, 74
elections, 3, 9, 13, 75
Elliott, Marianne, 49, 54
Emmet, Robert, 49
Emsley, Clive, 38, 41, 50, 65
England, 7, 8, 24, 38, 45, 48, 49, 50, 52, 60, 69, 77
Enquiry Concerning Political Justice, 17, 20
Erskine, Thomas, 38
Europe, 7, 8, 63
Evans, Thomas, 51, 52
Examiner, The, 71, 74
Example of France, A Warning to Britain, The, 30
Exeter, 36, 67

Falkner, Matthew, 40
Federal constitution, 6
Fitzgerald, Lord Edward, 46, 48
Flanders, 35
Flood, Henry, 7, 8
food prices, 9, 53
Ford, Richard, 37
Fox, Charles James, 29, 70
Foxite opposition, 21, 29
France, 6, 7, 8, 11, 19, 23, 24, 26, 29, 32, 34, 35, 37, 39, 42, 47, 48, 49, 51, 54, 56, 59, 60, 62, 64, 66, 67, 70, 71, 77
franchise, 3, 4, 5, 7, 9, 13, 15, 28, 46, 73, 76–7

Gales, Joseph, 11, 19, 40
Galloway, Alexander, 52
George III, 3
George, M. Dorothy, 41
Germany, 64
Gerrald, Joseph, 11, 21, 22, 38
Gifford, William, 30
Gill, Conrad, 56

85